WILD CATS

PAST & PRESENT

JOHN E. BECKER, PH.D.

ILLUSTRATIONS BY
MARK HALLETT

DARBY CREEK PUBLISHING

To all those individuals around the world who have devoted their lives to the preservation of wild cats, especially to the talented and concerned individuals at ISEC with whom I had the great privilege to work.

Cataloging-in-Publication

Becker, John E., 1942-.
Wild cats : past & present / by John E. Becker ; illustrations by Mark Hallett.
       p. ; cm.
ISBN 978-1-58196-052-5
Ages 11 and up.—Includes bibliographical references (p.) and index.—Summary: Not all cats are the playful pets we pamper; meet the wild cats. Wild cats have fascinated mankind for thousands of years. Each species has its own tale—from being worshiped to being feared as a ravaging monster. What is fiction and what is fact about these furry animals?
1. Felidae—Juvenile literature. [1. Cat family (Mammals)]
I. Title. II. Author. III. Ill.
QL737.C23 B43 2008
599.75 dc22
OCLC: 173185964

Darby Creek Publishing
7858 Industrial Parkway
Plain City, OH 43064
www.darbycreekpublishing.com

Printed in Italy

2 4 6 8 10 9 7 5 3 1

Photo Credits: cover: jungle © Justin Johnson/Dreamstime; tiger © Andrey Ushakov/Dreamstime. 5: ring-tailed cat © Gerard Lcacz/FLPA. 6: fossa © San Diego Zoo/Reuters/Landov. 11: Thylacine © Dave Watts. 18: jungle cat © Tzooka/Dreamstime; sand cat © Nancy Vandermey; black-footed cat © Terry Whittaker/FLPA; wild cat © Tony Hamblin/FLPA; oncilla © Terry Whittaker/FLPA. 19: Iberian lynx © Angel Sosa/Dreamstime; pampas cat © Frank W. Lane/FLPA; Geoffroy's cat © Terry Whittaker/FLPA; leopard cat © Johnny Lye/Dreamstime; flat-headed cat © Jim Sanderson; rusty-spotted cat © Terry Whittaker/FLPA; Asian golden cat © Supri/Reuters/Landov; jaguarundi © Nancy Vandermey; serval © David Hughes/Dreamstime; Andean mountain cat © E. Delgado, D. Berna, L. Villalba/PGA-Khastor; Pallas cat © Petr Masek/Dreamstime; African golden cat © Terry Whittaker/FLPA. 24: petroglyph © Paul Van Eykelen/Dreamstime. 25: cat pelts © Getty Images/Carl Iwasaki/Time Life Pictures Collection. 26: panthers © Joe Stone/Dreamstime. 28: Texas puma © Tim Chapman/MCT/Landov. 35: Geoffroy's cat © Terry Whittaker/FLPA; oncilla © Terry Whittaker/FLPA; jaguarundi © Nancy Vandermey; pampas cat © Frank W. Lane/FLPA; Andean mountain cat © E. Delgado, D. Berna, L. Villalba/PGA-Khastor. 37: jaguar © Michael Klenetsky/Dreamstime; leopard © Steffen Foerster/Dreamstime; leopard fur © David Davis/Dreamstime. 39: Geoffroy's cat © Terry Whittaker/FLPA. 41: Pallas' cat © Petr Masek/Dreamstime; Asian golden cat © Supri/Reuters/Landov; rusty-spotted cat © Terry Whittaker/FLPA; flat-headed cat © Jim Sanderson; leopard cat © Johnny Lye/Dreamstime; jungle cat © Tzooka/Dreamstime. 43: white tiger © Gino Santa Maria/Dreamstime. 44: leopard © Jim Clark/Dreamstime. 45: cheetah © Phil Berry/Dreamstime. 48: fishing cat © Olga Bogatyrenko/Dreamstime. Pallas' cat © Petr Masek/Dreamstime. 50: Iberian lynx © Angel Sosa/Dreamstime. 51: rusty-spotted cat © Terry Whittaker/FLPA; leopard cat © Johnny Lye/Dreamstime; jungle cat © Tzooka/Dreamstime. 52: serval © David Hughes/Dreamstime. 53: sand cat © Nancy Vandermey; African golden cat © Terry Whittaker/FLPA; wildcat © Tony Hamblin/FLPA; black-footed cat © Terry Whittaker/FLPA. 55: lioness © Marina Cano/Dreamstime. 56: cheetah © Keith Barlow/Dreamstime. 57: caracal © Vaslily Koval/Dreamstime. 58: serval cub © Olivia Falvey/Dreamstime; serval © David Bate/Dreamstime. 59: sand cat © Nancy Vandermey. 60: black-footed cat © Terry Whittaker/FLPA. 61: African wildcat © Malcom Schuyl/FLPA; African golden cat © Terry Whittaker/FLPA. 62: cat tablet © Aladin Abdel Naby/Reuters/Landov. 64: feral cats © Dwight Smith/Dreamstime. 68: cheetah mother and cubs © Juda Ngwenya/Landov. 70: flat-headed cat © Jim Sanderson. 72: Amur tiger © John Goodrich/WCS. All other photos from royalty-free stock sources are not credited.

CONTENTS

ANCIENT ANCESTORS

Crouch. Purr. Slink. Pounce. Stalk. Claw. Some words just go with cats—our pets or the wild ones. When you see a kitten creeping up on a feathered toy, you could just as well be looking at a lion cub stalking a grasshopper on the Serengeti. The slow, cautious movements and serious concentration are pretty much the same.

Is a ten-pound pet tabby found on the same family tree as a five-hundred-pound tiger? And what about the ancient ancestors of our modern cats? Are today's cats the descendants of saber-toothed cats—or did they come from a totally different kind of animal? You're about to discover the answers to these and many other questions about wild cats.

© Mark Hallett

DOGS AND CATS: A COMMON ANCESTOR?

Imagine Earth as it was sixty million years ago. The huge, thundering dinosaurs had disappeared, but the world was still a wild and dangerous place. In North America, the land was covered with thick forests that provided shelter for an amazing variety of weird-looking animals. Some of those animals were the hunted, while others stalked with deadly skill.

Prowling through the murky darkness were some of the earliest ancestors of the modern cat—a family of predators known as the miacids. Using their specialized teeth and claws, these fierce little predators hunted small prey. Miacids were small—not much bigger than overgrown alley cats—but they were excellent hunters that were extremely well suited for climbing trees.

Some scientists believe that miacids were the ancestors of both dogs and cats. These creatures had claws that retracted like cats' claws, but they also chewed their food with crushing molar teeth, just as dogs do. We know that some miacids were as large as coyotes.

Miacids disappeared long ago, but scientists tell us that our present-day ring-tailed cats (which really aren't cats at all) look quite similar to miacids.

Although larger, a miacid (*left*) looked very similar to today's ring-tailed cat (*right*), which is not really a cat at all.

BRANCHING OUT: DOGS AND CATS

Miacids had traits of both dogs and cats, so you shouldn't be surprised to learn that the miacids' family tree eventually split about 48 million year ago. From that time on, dogs and cats evolved separately.

The "dog" group, known as canids, was composed of wolf-like animals. The canids eventually became wolves, foxes, and dogs.

The other group, known as felids, included cat-like animals. Felids eventually became cats, hyenas, mongooses, and genets. Some of those animals are more closely related than others. Cats' closest relatives are genets and civets, animals that people often mistakenly call "cats."

canids
wolves
foxes
dogs

felids
cats
hyenas
mongooses
genets

The Past Meets the Present

You can get a glimpse into the past by looking at a fossa, a cat-like animal that lives in Madagascar. Experts believe fossas look similar to the very first kind of cat, *Proailurus*, which is shown on page 7.

Using their best detective work, scientists estimate that the first real cats pounced onto the scene approximately thirty million years ago. They may not have been here when the dinosaurs ruled the ancient reptile world, but the family roots of the cat are still fairly old.

The very first cat, *Proailurus*, was small. It weighed about twenty pounds and had short legs and a long body. *Proailurus* had retractable claws that allowed it to climb trees as easily as your neighborhood tomcat does.

Proailurus was just the beginning for cats. Next came the *Pseudaelurus*, which began stalking its prey about twenty million years ago. These nimble-footed predators also felt right at home up in the trees, even though they were larger than their earlier cousins— some as large as today's small pumas. But before they died out (about ten million years ago), *Pseudaelurus* gave rise to two major branches of the cat family tree. Scientists tell us that these mammals were not only the predecessors of saber-toothed cats, but they were also the direct ancestors of our modern house cats.

© Mark Hallett

Proailurus

SMILODON: THE SABER-TOOTHED CAT OF NORTH AND SOUTH AMERICA

Scientists can look at a pile of old bones and tell us a lot about the ancient animals. Take *Smilodon*, for example. Even though other kinds of saber-toothed animals roamed the earth long before *Smilodon* came along, scientists tell us saber-toothed cats had a long and impressive run at the top of the world's food chain. As a matter of fact, *Smilodon* prospered from about two million years ago until the last saber-toothed cats disappeared about ten thousand years ago.

Many *Smilodon* bones have been dug up in North America, but some *Smilodon* bones have also been discovered in South America. These fossils have given us valuable information about the shape and size of these amazing prehistoric cats.

The saber-toothed *Smilodon* died out about ten thousand years ago.

LA BREA TAR PITS

The Rancho La Brea Tar Pits in Los Angeles, California, stand out as a rich mine of *Smilodon* fossils. Usually called "tar pits," these Ice-Age areas of sticky ooze were, in fact, asphalt pools. (Asphalt is a naturally occurring substance, while tar is a man-made product.) The asphalt deposits at Rancho La Brea have offered up more than 1,200 individual Smilodons.

Paleontologists at Rancho La Brea have also uncovered the bones of hundreds of other animals that could have been meals for these saber-toothed cats. *Smilodons* were massive cats with enormous appetites, feasting on lions and many other kinds of mega-mammals of that day, such as bison, horses, antelope, deer, mammoths, and mastodons. (North America once was home to animals that were very similar to today's African lions.)

The *Smilodon*'s long, curved teeth would have been deadly weapons against almost any animal. Their saber teeth were not only large and sharp, but they also had finely notched edges like a saw blade, easily slicing through the flesh of a *Smilodon*'s victim.

Smilodon had short, powerful legs and a thick, muscular body. After studying the cats' bones at several different places, some scientists have decided that these animals may have lived and hunted together in social groups, or prides, like lions do today.

 # How Saber Teeth Worked

Have you ever tried to imagine how a saber-toothed cat used its deadly teeth to kill an animal? According to paleontologists, a saber-toothed cat probably had to creep close to its prey. Then, in the thick cover of trees or underbrush, it pounced on its unsuspecting victim and knocked it to the ground. Before the prey animal could free itself from the weight of the heavy cat, the predator would have used its long sword-like canine teeth to rip a hole in the animal's throat or inflict a gaping wound in the prey's underbelly. The saber-toothed cat most likely didn't plunge its saber teeth (up to seven inches long in some species) deep into its victim's body, because if it did, the cat would have put itself at risk, possibly breaking its teeth on a bone.

The only way saber-toothed cats could use their long teeth was by opening their jaws very, very wide. Think about how wide a lion opens its mouth when it yawns. Scientists tell us that modern lions open their jaws about 65 degrees when they sink their teeth into prey. Paleontologists calculate that *Smilodon fatalis*, the type of *Smilodon* found at Rancho La Brea, was capable of opening its jaws a full 95 degrees!

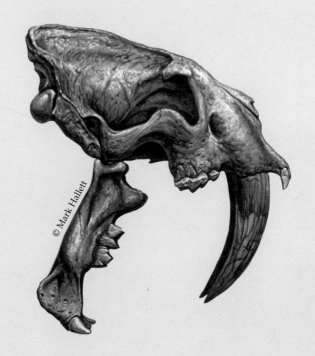

© Mark Hallett

HOMOTHERIUM: SABER-TOOTHED TERROR OF FOUR CONTINENTS

Another type of saber-toothed cat that lived from two million to ten thousand years ago was the *Homotherium*. These animals were a little smaller than the biggest saber-toothed cats, but their smaller size didn't keep them from getting around. *Homotherium*'s range extended from Alaska to Texas. They not only lived in North America, but also (like *Smilodon*) called Europe, Asia, and Africa home.

Homotherium stood as tall as a modern-day lion, but it was more streamlined than the stocky *Smilodon*, so it probably ran much faster. Some scientists think *Homotherium* could run sixty miles an hour while chasing prey in open areas like grasslands. Other clues tell us that these ferocious predators may have hunted in groups and that young mammoths were their favorite food.

The saber teeth of *Homotherium* were only about four inches long, not quite as long as *Smilodon*'s. But *Homotherium*'s saber teeth were much wider and had notches on both sides that allowed the teeth to cut like a steak knife through a meaty meal.

Homotherium

Most people know of only one kind of saber-toothed animal—the saber-toothed cat. But, according to Dr. Tom Rothwell of the American Museum of Natural History, at least four different types of meat-eating mammals developed saber teeth throughout ancient history.

The oldest saber-toothed animals made an appearance more than fifty million years ago, long before *Smilodon* came along. Known as creodonts, they were the earliest mammals to have saber-like canine teeth. Long before any cats were on the scene, one of the smaller creodonts, *Machaeroides simpsoni*, actually looked a little like a cat and had well-developed saber teeth.

Nimravids, the next saber-toothed animals to come along about forty million years ago, also looked like cats. Paleontologists refer to them as "false saber-toothed cats," because they were not the ancestors of either ancient saber-toothed cats or our modern cats.

Of all the saber-toothed animals that lived on Earth, nimravids had some of the most impressive saber teeth. The awesome *Barbourofelis* was the size of a modern lion and had a huge set of saber teeth that slid neatly into a long extension of its lower jaw.

One of the more unusual nimravids was more like a kangaroo than a wild cat, because it was a marsupial. *Thylacosmilus* was a marsupial predator, similar in size and appearance to a modern jaguar. It preyed on plant-eating animals in South America between eight and four million years ago. *Thylacosmilus* was actually a distant relative of the opossum, but unlike the opossum, *Thylacosmilus* didn't carry its babies in a pouch.

The now-extinct marsupial *Thylacine*, shown here, was also known as a Tasmanian tiger-wolf. It may have been a descendent of the *Thylacosmilus*.

11

Giant Mammals of the Ice Age

An ice age occurs when the planet's temperature drops significantly and ice covers much of its surface. During the last ice age, which ended about ten thousand years ago (a short time in geological terms), huge ice sheets, called glaciers, covered almost half of North America. Some of those glaciers extended as far south as present-day Missouri.

Geologically, the last ice age is known as the Pleistocene epoch. Because of the frigid climate, most of the mammals grew thick, hairy coats and were much larger than the mammals we see on Earth today. The ice and snow didn't slow them down. As a matter of fact, because so much of the earth's water was frozen in the glaciers, the level of the oceans was much lower than today. That gave the massive land mammals opportunities to explore. Many of them crossed over land or ice bridges from Europe and Asia into North America. Scientists think that people probably emigrated the same way, following the animal herds they hunted.

Most of the gigantic mammals of the last ice age aren't around anymore. But the prehistoric bones that paleontologists have painstakingly dug up, especially at places

Ancient bison and Columbian mammoths roamed much of North America during the last ice age.

like Rancho La Brea, help us see what ancient predators—like *Smilodon* and American lions—once hunted. Prey, like giant ancient bison (*Bison antiquus*)—which stood over six feet tall at the hump, weighed 3,500 pounds, and had enormous horns—would have been juicy dishes for *Smilodon*. American lions seemed to have more of a taste for western horses (*Equus occidentalis*).

The Columbian mammoth (*Mammuthus columbi*) and mastodon (*Mammut americanum*)—two extinct types of elephant—also would have been part of the big cats' diets. As found in La Brea, adult Columbian mammoths stood thirteen feet tall at the shoulder and had massive curved tusks that were up to sixteen feet long. The mastodons, also found in La Brea, were shaggier and smaller, standing about eight feet tall.

The largest animal ever trapped in the Rancho La Brea tar pits was a Columbian mammoth. By studying fossils, like the ones shown here, paleontologists have learned that mammoths had wide heads, a sloping back, and long, curved tusks, which were used for protection, to establish dominance, and to help gather food. Here's an interesting fact: Scientist have found that the inner surface of one tusk tended to be more worn than the other, meaning a mammoth could be "right-tusked" or "left-tusked."

As recently as ten thousand years ago, lions lived not only in Asia, Africa, and Europe, but also in North and South America. Like other predators, lions hungrily followed the herds of mammals that crossed over the land and ice bridges during the last ice age. But the American lions (*Panthera atrox*) probably didn't come from as far as Africa. Cave drawings by prehistoric artists clearly show that lions were living in caves across Europe and Asia at that time. Scientists tell us that those cave lions are the ones that found their way to the Americas.

Once they arrived, American lions spread across their new homeland. They lived as far north as Alaska, as far east as Florida, and as far south as Peru in South America (*see map*). Skeletons of more than eighty American lions have been recovered from Rancho La Brea alone.

From looking at American lion fossils, we know that they were closely related to modern African lions, even though male American lions were larger than their African relatives—and even larger than *Smilodon*. American lions had long legs and a skinnier body than African lions, too.

NORTH AMERICA

SOUTH AMERICA

The American lion once inhabited a wide territory: from Alaska to Florida to parts of South America. Today, no lions are found in the western hemisphere.

© Mark Hallett

WHY DID THESE ANCIENT CATS DISAPPEAR?

What caused the extinction of so many species of wildlife at the end of the last ice age? This is still one of the greatest unsolved mysteries of all time.

Some scientists think that people helped wipe them out by hunting them into extinction, but other scientists have their doubts about this theory. These experts like to point out that people have coexisted with large animals, especially in Africa, for thousands of years and that most of those animals have not disappeared.

According to paleontologist Russ Graham of Pennsylvania State University, predators like *Smilodons* and American lions may not have been able to change their eating habits once their food sources became scarce. Earth's climate changed rapidly at the end of the last ice age—in less than one human lifetime. When things warmed up, the big plant-eating animals were trapped in smaller and smaller areas, and the foods they ate disappeared. As the plant-eaters died off, the large meat-eaters had less to consume, causing them to have fewer and fewer babies. Before long, both the large prey animals and the large predators headed down the same road as the dinosaurs. Similarly, loss of habitat is a main reason so many species are nearing extinction today.

© Mark Hallett

As their food sources died out, the ancient wild cats, like the *Homotherium* shown here, slowly starved to death.

WILD CATS AROUND THE WORLD

Sometimes the names we give to animals and plants can be confusing. For example, people have called bobcats (*Lynx rufus*) by many different names. Often, bobcats are just called wildcats, but in some places they're called red lynx or bay lynx, even though they are the same animal. All of those are "common names" for the same animal.

Scientists use a system that helps eliminate the confusion. This system, called taxonomy, is organized from general to specific. First, the **kingdom** is identified based on what kind of creature it is: plant (Plantae), animal (Animalia), fungus (Fungi), or one of another two

or three categories. If the kingdom is Animalia, next comes one question: Does this animal have a vertebra (backbone)? If so, the **phylum** is Chordata, meaning "cord," as in spinal cord.

Let's continue by using the bobcat as our example. Its kingdom is Animalia; its phylum is Chordata. Bobcats are mammals, animals that give birth to live young, nurse their young with milk, and have hair, so it belongs in the **class** Mammalia. A class is then divided into smaller groups called orders. Within the class Mammalia, the **order** Carnivora is comprised of all meat-eating animals, including the bobcat. Different kinds of carnivores are next split into families, one of which is a group only for cats—both wild and domestic cats—the **family** Felidae. (Dogs belong in the family Canidae.)

One interesting thing about taxonomy is that it doesn't stay the same forever. When new scientific discoveries are made, the taxonomy can change. Recently, as a result of new knowledge, scientists have subdivided the family Felidae into three subfamilies: Acinonychinae, Pantherinae, and Felinae. Next, **subfamilies** (or families, if there are no subfamilies) are divided into groups of animals that have similar characteristics. Each of these groups is called a **genus**. All lynx, including bobcats, have ear tufts at the top of their large ears, so they're grouped together in one genus: *Lynx*.

Each genus is divided into individual **species**. All bobcats, whether they live in Florida or in Canada, are in the same species, *Lynx rufus* (meaning "red lynx"). Obviously, the bobcats living in Florida are a little different from the bobcats living in British Columbia, Canada, so they're divided one last time into subspecies. The subspecies of bobcat living in Florida is *Lynx rufus floridanus*, while the subspecies of bobcat in British Columbia is *Lynx rufus fasciatus*. The taxonomy chart below shows the taxonomy of the bobcat, and on the following pages you will find all thirty-six known species of wild cats in the world today.

Taxonomy of the Bobcat

A bobcat (*Lynx rufus*)

KINGDOM	Animalia
PHYLUM	Chordata
CLASS	Mammalia
ORDER	Carnivora
FAMILY	Felidae
SUBFAMILY	Felinae
GENUS	*Lynx*
SPECIES	*rufus*

SUBFAMILIES OF FAMILY FELIDAE

1. cheetah
2. tiger
3. lion
4. jaguar
5. leopard
6. snow leopard
7. clouded leopard
8. marbled cat
9. Chinese mountain cat
10. jungle cat
11. sand cat
12. black-footed cat
13. wild cat
14. ocelot
15. oncilla (or tigrina)
16. margay
17. Canada lynx
18. Eurasian lynx

Subfamily: Acinonychinae

	Genus	Species	Common Name
1	*Acinonyx*	*jubatus*	cheetah

Subfamily: Pantherinae

	Genus	Species	Common Name
2	*Panthera*	*tigris*	tiger
3	*Panthera*	*leo*	lion
4	*Panthera*	*onca*	jaguar
5	*Panthera*	*pardus*	leopard
6	*Uncia*	*uncia*	snow leopard
7	*Neofelis*	*nebulosa*	clouded leopard
8	*Pardofelis*	*marmorata*	marbled cat

Subfamily: Felinae

	Genus	Species	Common Name
9	*Felis*	*bieti*	Chinese mountain cat
10	*Felis*	*chaus*	jungle cat
11	*Felis*	*margarita*	sand cat
12	*Felis*	*nigripes*	black-footed cat
13	*Felis*	*silvestrus*	wild cat
14	*Leopardus*	*paradalis*	ocelot

* Due to the rarity of some species, photos are unavailable.

Subfamily: Felinae (continued)

	GENUS	SPECIES	COMMON NAME
15	*Leopardus*	*tigrinus*	oncilla (or tigrina)
16	*Leopardus*	*wiedii*	margay
17	*Lynx*	*canadensis*	Canada lynx
18	*Lynx*	*lynx*	Eurasian lynx
19	*Lynx*	*pardinus*	Iberian lynx
20	*Lynx*	*rufus*	bobcat
21	*Oncifelis*	*colocolo*	pampas cat
22	*Oncifelis*	*geoffroi*	Geoffroy's cat
23	*Oncifelis*	*guigna*	guigna (or kodkod)
24	*Prionailurus*	*bengalensis*	leopard cat
25	*Prionailurus*	*planiceps*	flat-headed cat
26	*Prionailurus*	*rubiginosus*	rusty-spotted cat
27	*Prionailurus*	*viverrinus*	fishing cat
28	*Catopuma*	*badia*	bay cat
29	*Catopuma*	*temminckii*	Asian golden cat
30	*Caracal*	*caracal*	caracal
31	*Herpailurus*	*yagouaroundi*	jaguarundi
32	*Leptailurus*	*serval*	serval
33	*Oreailurus*	*jacobita*	Andean mountain cat
34	*Otocologus*	*manul*	Pallas' cat
35	*Profelis*	*aurata*	African golden cat
36	*Puma*	*concolor*	puma

19 Iberian lynx

20 bobcat

21 pampas cat

22 Geoffroy's cat

23 guigna (or kodkod) — photo unavailable *

24 leopard cat

25 flat-headed cat

26 rusty-spotted cat

27 fishing cat

28 bay cat — photo unavailable *

29 Asian golden cat

30 caracal

31 jaguarundi

32 serval

33 Andean mountain cat

34 Pallas' cat

35 African golden cat

36 puma

WILD CATS OF NORTH AMERICA

Thirty-six species of wild cats live in the world today, and six of those live in North America, the world's third-largest continent that includes Canada, the U.S., Mexico, and Central America. Most people can name the puma, bobcat, and Canada lynx, but the jaguars, jaguarundis, and ocelots are less well known because they are so rare in the U.S. Those three cats are more commonly found in Mexico and Central America.

Of the North American cats, pumas are probably the best known. You might know them by other names: cougar, mountain lion, or Florida panther, common names for the same species. Pumas are the second-largest wild cats in this part of the world, after the jaguar, often weighing more than one hundred pounds. These big cats make their homes throughout a huge territory that includes the western United States and Canada, southern Florida, Mexico, Central America, and South America.

The other common North American wild cats—bobcats and Canada lynx—are quite a bit smaller than pumas, usually weighing

around twenty pounds. Bobcats are found across southern Canada, throughout most of the United States, and into central Mexico. Canada lynx, on the other hand, live where the climate is colder, like Alaska and some northern areas of the United States. But, as

you can guess from their name, they mainly roam across Canada.

Sadly, all of the species of wild cats in North America are fewer in number than they used to be, mainly because they have been hunted for hundreds of years. The good news is that they are still here and that measures are being taken to protect the North American wild cats.

bobcat (*Lynx rufus*)

puma (*Puma concolor*)

Canada lynx (*Lynx canadensis*)

AMERICA'S CAT: THE PUMA

Imagine a kind of wild cat that once roamed freely from the Yukon region in northern Canada to the southern tip of South America and from the Atlantic Ocean to the Pacific Ocean. The puma, *Puma concolor*, wandered over that entire territory before European settlers arrived.

In 1502, Christopher Columbus reported seeing a lion in Central America. When other Europeans came to the Americas, they also saw big wild cats that looked like the man-eating lions that had been known to attack people in Africa and had once terrorized their ancestors in Europe.

Early settlers told stories of horrible beasts that attacked innocent people and savagely tore them to pieces. Some of the tales described bloodthirsty pumas snatching babies from their cribs, ambushing hunters as they walked through the forest, and slaughtering farm animals.

Unfortunately for the pumas, the stories of their cruel attacks were greatly exaggerated. Still, people believed that the stories were true. Settlers tried to wipe out the pumas—and nearly succeeded.

Scientists tell us that pumas are usually shy and normally don't attack unless they're being chased or are protecting their young. Most Americans are now more understanding of pumas' habits, so fewer are being killed, allowing pumas to make a comeback.

Today, pumas still have the widest range of any wild cat in the Americas, but the

These pumas show some of the varieties of coat colors that the species can display.

pumas living in North America now are mostly limited to the western parts of the continent. Exactly where they live in Mexico, Central, and South America is a mystery, but scientists believe they probably hide out in much smaller areas than they did even one hundred years ago.

Pumas are some of the most adaptable animals in the world. They can live quite nicely in extremely different habitats—from windy mountain ridges to sweltering lowland swamps, from bone-dry deserts to dripping-wet tropical rainforests.

What do these pouncing predators look like? Adult pumas look a lot like female lions with a coat of only one color. The coat color can range from tan to reddish-brown to yellow-gray and even black. A puma's tail is almost as long as its body. A male puma can be as much as thirty inches tall at the shoulder—and a really big male can weigh as much as two hundred pounds and measure more than eight feet from his nose to the tip of his tail.

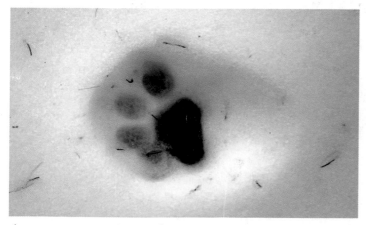

A cougar pawprint in the snow

A Cat of Many Names

The scientific name for a puma, Puma concolor, means "cat of one color," one scientific name that makes sense! Because pumas roamed over such a gigantic territory, people from different areas gave them several common names. Here are just a few:

- **Puma** was a Peruvian word that meant "a powerful animal." The Incas showed their respect for pumas as powerful predators.

- Another name for the puma, **cougar**, originally came from the native Brazilian word for jaguar.

- The first Europeans to see pumas thought they were female lions, so they called them **lions**, or **mountain lions**. (They must have wondered why they never saw any male lions.)

- In New England, an area with plenty of mountains, people gave pumas the name **catamount**, which is short for "cat of the mountains."

- One of the vocalizations (sounds) that pumas make during mating season is a high-pitched sound, kind of like a woman screaming. This led to the name **screamer**.

- Some pumas are all black. So, as you might imagine, they were called **panthers**. In Florida, pumas have always been known as **Florida panthers**, even though no black ones exist today.

Most Native American tribes believed that their wild neighbors—pumas and other wildlife—should be respected. For centuries, natives watched pumas stalking their prey and decided that pumas were great hunters that deserved to be admired for their ability to survive.

Some tribes even worshipped pumas as gods and honored the cats with colorful ceremonies. Even today, the Hopi tribe of the American Southwest considers the puma to be a very important symbol. Pumas are thought of as fearless animals whose great strength protects the tribe. In return, members of the tribe worship the puma god. Ceremonial dances call up the spirit of the puma during times of need.

But not every tribe worshipped pumas. Some tribes stole the pumas' kills so they'd have enough food to eat. In ancient Peru, the Incas organized huge circle hunts to round up and kill pumas and other animals. Because the cats preyed on the same animals that the Incas hunted for food, the people tried to eliminate the cats.

Other tribes hunted pumas, too, but they didn't consider the puma an enemy. Usually, the reason for hunting a puma was to obtain a sacred part, such as its teeth or claws, providing a warrior protection from harm. Some also believed the bones could prevent the sick from dying.

This Native American petroglyph (rock picture) found at the Petroglyph National Monument in Albuquerque, New Mexico, shows a cat-like animal.

As Europeans spread out across North America, they took their dislike of pumas with them. In the 1500s, for example, Jesuit priests in California offered local natives a bull as a prize for each puma they killed. Owning a bull was important, so despite their tribal beliefs, the Native Americans helped thin out the California puma population. In eastern America, as early as 1680, rewards called bounties were offered for killing. Soon, pioneers paid bounties for dead pumas wherever they settled.

Over the next two centuries, pumas slowly disappeared from the eastern U.S. and the eastern provinces of Canada. The last puma in Vermont was killed in 1881, and ten years later, the last indigenous puma in Pennsylvania was killed. By 1900, pumas were practically eliminated east of the Mississippi River, except for a few that survived in the swamps of southern Florida.

Wiping out pumas in the East was one thing, but how could pumas disappear from the wide-open spaces of the American West? If you think about ranches with thousands of cattle, you'll understand. As long as pumas had plenty of bison, elk, and deer to eat, everything was okay. But once those animals began to disappear, pumas started raiding herds of cattle and sheep. As you can imagine, it didn't take long for the ranchers to declare war on pumas. Pumas were shot, trapped, and poisoned wherever ranchers found them. Then, in 1915, the U.S. government joined the ranchers by hiring hunters to kill pumas and other varmints (dangerous wild animals). In 1931, a government agency, Animal Damage Control (ADC), joined the fight. From 1937 to 1970, ADC killed more than 7,000 pumas. Between 1918 and 1947, about 2,400 pumas were killed in the state of Arizona alone. Today predator-control programs are still in effect in most western states.

Hunters killed wild cats for many reasons, including for their furs.

The Endangered Species Act has helped many species of wild cats, including Florida panthers, shown above.

THE BATTLE TO SAVE PUMAS

We definitely know one thing about pumas: They're survivors! No matter what people have tried to do to them, pumas have shown an amazing ability to endure. Thankfully, during the twentieth century, people started to figure out that wild animals needed protection. Early in that century, several national parks, wildlife preserves, and other protected areas for wildlife were set up around the country. Then in 1973, the Endangered Species Act (ESA) was passed to help protect our wild animals from extinction. Today, three subspecies of puma are listed as endangered and are protected from being hunted: the eastern puma, the Florida panther, and the Costa Rican puma.

The idea that predators are an important part of a well-balanced ecosystem is starting to make sense to people—and that's good for pumas, too. Most western states and Canadian provinces have changed the status of pumas from "varmints" to "game animals." That might not seem to be much of a difference, but this is an important change. You see, anybody can kill a varmint at any time for any reason, but game animals can legally be hunted only at certain times and in certain places. Also, a limit is set on the number of those animals that can be killed. The only state in the U.S. that still lists the pumas as varmints is Texas, where ranchers have significant political power.

Why would anyone be in favor of people killing pumas whenever they want? The main reason is that the wild cats kill livestock. Others point out, however, that in both Colorado and Wyoming, ranchers are paid for animals that are killed by pumas. Very little money is paid out each year by those states, indicating that the number of animals killed by pumas is small.

 # Puma Attacks

The good news is that since pumas have been given protection, their numbers have slowly gone up. The bad news is that the number of people living in puma territory has also increased—a lot. The chance of people running into pumas when they go jogging, hiking, or sightseeing is greater, as well.

According to Dr. Paul Beier, a Northern Arizona University professor who investigated mountain-lion attacks that occurred between 1890 and 1990, fifty-one attacks were reported during those one hundred years. But since 1991, more than seventy additional attacks have been reported. Most attacks have happened to children; thankfully those rarely resulted in death. Despite the increase in the number of reported attacks, scientists remind us that most pumas are shy and usually try to avoid people whenever they can.

Should people think about puma attacks before they venture on foot into those territories? Absolutely! In case you're out in puma country, especially at twilight or dusk, here are a few important tips to remember:

- The best way to avoid an attack is to walk with other people.

- Never run when you see a puma. Running away or kneeling down will encourage a puma to attack, increasing the chances of serious injury.

- Always talk or make noise as you are walking. This gives a puma plenty of time to get away.

- If a puma does appear, grownups should immediately pick up children who are with them.

- Everyone should stand as tall as possible, make lots of loud noises, face the puma (never lose eye contact), and fight back if it attacks.

Some areas provide warnings that mountain lions (pumas) are nearby.

A little more than a hundred years ago, Florida panthers, *Puma concolor coryi*, were living not only in Florida, but also across the American Southeast from Louisiana to North Carolina to Florida. Today, they're among the rarest animals living in America. Scientists believe that these wild cats were never very numerous, but by the middle of the twentieth century, Florida panthers had all but disappeared from their former territory, except for a few that managed to hold out in south Florida.

U.S. federal and state agencies and private conservation groups are working hard to keep Florida panthers around. One strategy is to greatly increase protected areas for the panthers and other animals. Over the past twenty-five years, hundreds of thousands of acres have been set aside in south Florida as protected panther habitat.

Another strategy is to cut down on the number of panthers killed on highways, the leading cause of death of these wild cats. To help eliminate vehicle/ panther collisions, some roads in south Florida are now fenced off, which forces panthers and other animals to go from one side of the highway to the other through "wildlife underpasses." And it works! So far, no panthers have been hit by cars where these underpasses are available.

Another important approach was put in place in 1995. Eight female pumas from Texas were released in Florida in hopes that more panthers would be born. Mark Lotz, panther biologist with the Florida Fish & Wildlife Conservation Commission, explains: "Since Texas pumas were introduced, they've bred with Florida panthers, helping to eliminate problems caused by inbreeding. One of those problems, an inability to fight off diseases, has been corrected."

Because Texas pumas are a different subspecies from Florida panthers, you might

The Texas puma, shown here, is helping save the Florida panthers from extinction.

think that mixing the genes of the two would cause the Florida panther to disappear. But Mark Lotz explains that the two subspecies used to mix naturally before they were separated by habitat destruction caused by expanding human populations. Because only a tiny number of Texas pumas have bred with Florida panthers, the gene flow from one subspecies to the other is approximately the same as it has been in the past, ensuring that Florida panthers will continue to be a distinct subspecies.

RETURN OF THE EASTERN PUMAS

The last eastern puma was thought to have disappeared many years ago, but sightings of pumas throughout the eastern U.S. and Canada have sometimes been reported. For a long time, wildlife officials insisted that the reports weren't true because no living or dead pumas were ever presented as proof. But as reports continued to come in, some experts, including Canadian wildlife official Bruce S. Wright, began to wonder if there might be some truth to the claims. In his 1972 book, *The Eastern Panther: A Question of Survival*, Mr. Wright gave evidence to support his belief that a small number of pumas had survived in northeastern North America.

Many more sightings have been reported since Wright's book was published. Recently some of the puma sightings have been confirmed, not only in the Northeast, but also in the midwestern states of Nebraska, Iowa, Missouri, Arkansas, and Illinois. The sightings may be a sign that young western pumas are coming eastward in the United States as they seek new territories. This makes sense because we know that the number of western pumas is increasing. Sightings of pumas in Massachusetts, New York, Pennsylvania, and West Virginia may also be a clue that pumas are moving across Canada and then down from Canada into the eastern U.S. through forested corridors.

A young eastern puma peeks out from a tree.

BOBCATS: NATURE'S TOUGH LITTLE SURVIVORS

Have you heard the expression, "He could whip his weight in wildcats"? It was a popular saying that pioneers used to describe a really tough person. The "wildcat" they were talking about was a bobcat. Pound for pound, bobcats (*Lynx rufus*) are some of the most aggressive animals in North America. Weighing between fifteen and thirty-five pounds, these feisty little predators are just a bit bigger than a large house cat, but they're by no means gentle pets.

Early settlers tried to get rid of bobcats in the same ways they tried to eliminate pumas. From the time Europeans first arrived until the middle of the twentieth century, the number of bobcats slowly decreased across most of North America. Because they're small and good at avoiding people, bobcats have been able to survive. Some wildlife biologists who admire bobcats have compared them to the champion canine survivors—coyotes.

Like coyotes, bobcats are not picky when it comes to prey. Here are some facts about bobcat food:

- **Size is no object**. Hunters have reported seeing bobcats taking down full-grown deer.

- **Bobcats help farmers**. Bobcats seldom kill domestic livestock. Much more often, they eat rabbits, rats and mice that can do serious damage to a farmer's crops.

- **A bobcat's diet is varied**. Because they're opportunistic hunters—meaning they eat anything they can catch—bobcats eat all kinds of things: insects, salamanders, fish, birds, bats, snakes, and many different mammals.

A bobcat will eat most anything, including (in this case) a pheasant.

Since the 1970s when laws to protect bobcats were passed and stronger hunting regulations were put in place, bobcat populations have increased considerably. Getting exact bobcat numbers is almost impossible, but experts believe that these adaptable felines are no longer in trouble in most places where they live.

The Return of the Bobcats: Cumberland Island, Georgia

In the early part of the twentieth century, the very last bobcat on Cumberland Island was killed. The small island, located off the coast of Georgia, had once been home to bears, wolves, pumas, and bobcats, but by 1908 all of those predators were long gone. For the next eighty years, plant-eating animals, especially white-tailed deer, continued to increase in numbers, even though people hunted them. When scientists checked out the island in the 1980s, they discovered that the deer were eating far too many of the plants that the island needed in order to remain environmentally healthy. For example, the sprouts of oak trees were being gobbled up, and eventually oak trees would disappear from the island.

In 1988, scientists from the University of Georgia decided to try to put the island in balance again. Their plan was to bring bobcats back in the hopes that they'd eat enough deer and other plant-eating animals to stop the damage. The crew went to the mainland of Georgia, rounded up thirty-two bobcats, and put radio collars on them so they could keep track of the cats. Once the bobcats were turned loose, the scientists started collecting information about the cats' diets.

Not surprisingly, the bobcats were eating deer—lots of deer! Smaller deer herds caused the deer to be healthier than they had been in a long time. The study also showed that the number of oak sprouts had increased and that they were growing much faster than before.

Dr. Robert Warren, head of the research team, explains: "By bringing back a natural deer predator, we were able to re-establish a greater balance between the predator and prey species, which then also benefited the plant growth on the island. To this day, offspring of the bobcats originally released in 1988 and 1989 are still spotted on Cumberland Island."

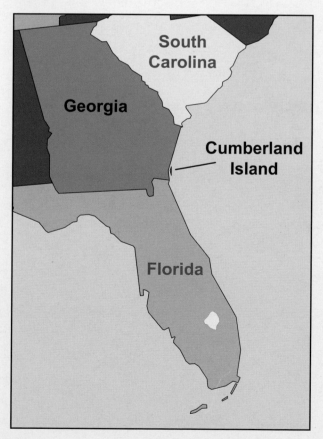

THE ELUSIVE CANADA LYNX

It's easy to confuse the Canada lynx (*Lynx canadensis*) with the bobcat (*Lynx rufus*), but they're definitely not the same species. As you might guess, the Canada lynx lives mainly across Canada, but these medium-sized fur balls are also found in eight northern U.S. states: Washington, Colorado, Wyoming, Montana, Minnesota, Maine, Michigan, and Alaska (where there are a lot of them). Sometimes Canada lynx also wander into Utah, New Hampshire, and Wisconsin. These animals aren't in as much danger as some other wild cats, but they are listed as a threatened species in the lower forty-eight states.

At first glance, a Canada lynx seems to be bigger than a bobcat. That's because of its fluffy fur coat, which in the winter is usually gray with speckles of black. During the summer months, the Canada lynx has a much shorter reddish-brown coat. It also has a short tail with a black tip, and it has big, round eyes that are especially suited for hunting at night. Facial ruff—which looks like extra-long whiskers and sideburns—helps keep snow and ice off the lynx's face. All species of lynx have ear tufts (hairs that point up from their large ears), and the Canada lynx's are especially long.

Snowshoe hares are by far the favorite food of the lynx. When the hare population is low, Canada lynx will expand their menus and eat other animals, such as birds and small mammals. When the snow is especially deep, these cats may kill young deer, moose, or elk—a tall order for such a small cat.

Both the Canada lynx (*left*) and bobcat (*right*) have tufted ears, but they are different in many other ways. Compare their coats, tails, feet and facial ruff.

Not many predators depend on one kind of prey animal as much as the Canada lynx depends on the snowshoe hare. We know this because one of the world's top fur-trapping outfits, the Hudson's Bay Company of Canada, has been keeping trapping records for more than two hundred years, and they've discovered something interesting. Their records show that whenever snowshoe hare populations go up, Canada lynx populations go up, too.

This connection was interesting to scientists, especially when people became worried about wild cats disappearing around the world. When scientists studied the records, they saw that over a period of about ten years, the number of snowshoe hares across Canada went way up, but then the number dropped. Over the same ten-year period, lynx numbers also went up and then crashed. This fascinating cycle has repeated itself approximately every ten years, decade after decade.

According to Dr. Ron Moen, who studies Canada lynx for the Natural Resources Research Institute at the University of Minnesota Duluth, that pattern began to change in Minnesota during the 1980s. "Lynx and snowshoe hare populations usu-ally cycle on about a ten-year interval," he explains, "but in Minnesota at least, snowshoe hare populations didn't recover from the low point in their cycle in the 1980s. Since then, Canada lynx sightings in Minnesota have been relatively rare—until recently."

All this information has been used to help Canada lynx by allowing scientists to predict when crashes in lynx populations will occur. State wildlife agencies can limit the trapping of Canada lynx during the low points of their population cycles, which, in turn, will help ensure Canada lynx won't be over hunted in the future.

This snowshoe hare has its winter coat. In spring, its coloring will be a common brownish gray.

CENTRAL AND SOUTH AMERICAN WILD CATS

As we learned in the previous section, the wild cats of North America include those that make their homes in Mexico and Central America. Some of the wild cats you are about to meet in this section can also be found in Mexico and Central America, but not in the U.S. or Canada. Known as Latin America, this largely Spanish-speaking area includes Mexico, Central America, and the continent of South America.

The mountains and rainforests of Latin America provide the habitat for these nine species of wild cats. The jaguar (*Panthera onca*) is the largest of those species, weighing as much as three hundred pounds. The smallest species—oncillas (*Leopardus tigrinus*) and guignas (*Oncifelis guigna*), also called kodkods—are so tiny that if you saw one, you might think it was a very small house cat. Jaguarundis (*Herpailurus yagouaroundi*) are small, too, and they look so much like otters that people sometimes call them "otter cats."

In this section, you will discover the beautiful wild cats of Latin America.

puma
(Puma concolor)

jaguar
(Panthera onca)

ocelot
(Leopardus paradalis)

margay
(Leopardus wiedii)

Geoffroy's cat
(Oncifelis geoffroi)

photo
unavailable *

guigna or kodkod
(Oncifelis guigna)

oncilla
(Leopardus tigrinus)

jaguarundi
(Herpailurus yagouaroundi)

pampas cat
(Oncifelis colocolo)

Andean mountain cat
(Oreailurus jacobita)

* Due to the rarity of some species, photos are unavailable.

THE JAGUAR: SYMBOL OF POWER AND MIGHT

The third-largest wild cat in the world makes its home in Latin America: the jaguar (*Panthera onca*). On the entire planet, only tigers and lions are bigger than jaguars. Not only are jaguars big, but they also are incredibly strong. With huge skulls and thick neck muscles, jaguars have the most powerful jaws for their size of any cat in the world—strong enough to crush the shell of a four-hundred-pound sea turtle. Jaguars are also very good swimmers and are bold enough in the water to attack a caiman (a relative of the alligator and crocodile).

Jaguars once lived in the midsection of North America and throughout Central and South America. The awesome power of the jaguar must have made quite an impression on the native people. They believed that jaguars were related to the gods. For example, the Mayas of Central America believed that a jaguar god ruled the underworld. They felt that the jaguar, or balam, was responsible for the sun passing from the sky to its resting place beneath the earth each night and believed that when they laid a jaguar's skin on the ground, the stars and the heavens were spread out before them.

Unfortunately, the jaguar's territory is nowhere near as large as it used to be. As people continue to cut down the trees of Latin American rainforests and destroy the jaguars' habitat, these amazing predators have fewer and fewer places to live. Jaguars are also killed for attacking farmers' livestock. Although they're officially listed as threatened throughout their range, jaguars are only treated as endangered in certain parts of that range.

Some scientists are optimistic that jaguars can survive into the future. According to jaguar expert Alan Rabinowitz, "Despite the killing and loss of habitat, there are some very good populations of jaguars still existing, and with protection they have a very good chance of doing well."

In the early 1980s, Dr. Rabinowitz went to Belize for the first time to study jaguars—and discovered they were disappearing. So he convinced the government of Belize to set aside a protected area of land as the world's first jaguar preserve. Today he is the Executive Director of Science and Exploration at the Wildlife Conservation Society, where he also runs the "Save the Jaguar" campaign, which focuses on preserving jaguars from Mexico to Argentina.

"Save the Jaguar" has already made good progress in setting aside more protected areas for jaguars, as well as in educating people about the important role that jaguars play in a healthy environment. But more work needs to be done. (You can check out some conservation projects for wild cats at the back of this book.)

 "Spot"light on Jaguars, Leopards, and Cheetahs (and a Note about Panthers)

If you have trouble telling jaguars, leopards, and cheetahs apart, you're not alone. According to Pat Calahan, head keeper of cats at the Cincinnati Zoo & Botanical Garden, people often get them mixed up.

To make things even more confusing, a lot of us call any big cat a "panther," especially if it's all black. The truth is, there's no such thing as a panther. This common name for a big cat came about as a shortened version of the genus *Panthera*, which includes tigers, lions, leopards, and jaguars. (Oh, and black leopards or jaguars are not missing their spots, either. These animals are melanistic, meaning their coloring is extremely dark, but they do have spots, which can be barely seen from certain angles.)

Here's how to tell these spotted cats apart:

Jaguars are stockier than leopards. They have huge heads and gold to rusty-red coats. The jaguar's coat also has dark spots that form circles (called rosettes) that have one or two spots in the middle.

Leopards have shorter legs; fuller, more muscular bodies; and rosettes, especially in the middle of the body.

Cheetahs are built similar to a greyhound dog, thin and streamlined, with a small head and solid black spots sprinkled across a tawny-yellow coat. They also have black "tear" stripes that run from the corner of the eyes to the mouth.

Two of a Kind: Ocelots and Margays

Did you ever notice that nature some-times repeats itself? Take ocelots (*Leopardus paradalis*) and margays (*Leopardus wiedii*), for example. These two Latin American wild cats look almost exactly the same, and they even live in the same places. But they're different sizes.

Ocelots are the second-largest spotted cats in Latin America, but they're much, much smaller than jaguars. A big male ocelot can weigh more than thirty pounds, while a female can weigh as little as fifteen pounds. Ocelots have shorthaired coats that are heavily spotted. The spots are generally dark, often running in lines across the back and sides. An ocelot has enormous eyes, which help it have keen vision when it hunts at night. And although ocelots are good at climbing trees, they usually hunt small mammals and lizards on the ground.

Based on coat markings, it's hard to tell the difference between margays and ocelots. But margays are smaller and not as stocky as ocelots. Male margays only weigh up to nine pounds. If you think an ocelot has big eyes, wait until you see a margay's! A margay also has a thicker fur coat and a longer tail, but otherwise it's a smaller version of its larger cousin. Unlike ocelots, margays love to spend

The ocelot (*above*) and the margay (*below*) look very much alike and even live in the same areas.

time in the trees, where they hunt birds, small mammals, lizards, and insects at night.

Unfortunately, during the twentieth century both of these cat species were killed to make fur coats for people. Today, all spotted wild cats are protected by international laws, but an illegal fur trade continues to thrive in some places.

CAT OF THE MOUNTAINS: THE GEOFFROY'S CAT

Someday when you're a famous scientist and you discover an animal that no one knew existed, other scientists may name that animal after you. That is how many animals and plants get their names. For instance, the Geoffroy's cat (*Oncifelis geoffroi*), another small wildcat found only in Latin America, was named after nineteenth-century French naturalist, Geoffroy St. Hilaire.

If you went to South America and came across a Geoffroy's cat, you'd probably think it was someone's escaped pet cat. But if you tried to pick it up, you'd be sorry, because these house-cat-sized predators (four to thirteen pounds) are extremely wild. Geoffroy's cats can be found pouncing on unsuspecting prey in the Andes Mountain regions of Bolivia, Argentina, and neighboring countries. There, people call them *gato montes* (Spanish for "mountain cat").

Geoffroy's cats love to eat fish, so they spend a lot of time around streams and lakes. They're also the cat family's version of a prairie dog because of their habit of standing on their back legs and scanning the horizon for prey.

Like ocelots and margays, thousands of Geoffroy's cats have been killed for their beautiful spotted fur coats. Despite modern laws, they're still victims of illegal fur trading.

WILD CATS OF EUROPE, ASIA, & THE MIDDLE EAST

Eurasia—Europe, Asia, and the Middle East—stretches from Portugal and Spain in the west to Russia in the east, and from the Siberian region of Russia in the north through Malaysia in the south. It's easy to see how that part of the world could be home to many wild animals, including an assortment of wild cats.

Some Eurasian cats look like cats from other parts of the world. The beautiful Eurasian lynx looks quite similar to the Canada lynx. More often, though, the wild cats of Eurasia are unlike any others.

One reason they're unique is that they have developed in a way that allows them to survive in the extreme habitats where they live. Some of these environments make it tough to live as a predator—places like steamy tropical jungles, snow-capped mountains, and brutally hot deserts. Eurasian wild cats are some of the most adaptable animals found anywhere on Earth.

tiger
(*Panthera tigris*)

leopard
(*Panthera pardus*)

cheetah
(*Acinonyx jubatus*)

snow leopard
(*Uncia uncia*)

fishing cat
(*Prionailurus viverrinus*)

Pallas' cat
(*Octocologus manul*)

Eurasian lynx
(*Lynx lynx*)

Iberian lynx
(*Lynx pardinus*)

clouded leopard
(*Neofelis nebulosa*)

photo
unavailable *

Chinese mountain cat
(*Felis bieti*)

photo
unavailable *

marbled cat
(*Pardofelis marmorata*)

Asian golden cat
(*Catopuma temminckii*)

rusty-spotted cat
(*Prionailurus rubiginosus*)

flat-headed cat
(*Prionailurus planiceps*)

leopard cat
(*Prionailurus bengalensis*)

jungle cat
(*Felis chaus*)

photo
unavailable *

Bornean bay cat
(*Catopuma badia*)

* Due to the rarity of some species, photos are unavailable.

Try to imagine what it would be like to come face to face with the biggest, baddest wild cat of them all. If you think I'm talking about a lion, think again—the true king of the wild cats is the tiger.

Tigers are bigger than lions, weighing in at well over four hundred pounds, and some can even weigh more than seven hundred pounds! These gigantic hunters are also unbelievably strong and can run faster than the fastest track star. Their combination of power and speed makes these super-sized kitties the ultimate predators. Tigers are not only the largest wild cats living today, but they may be the largest cats to ever live on Earth.

What makes tigers even more impressive is how well they do in some of the world's toughest environments. Amur tigers (*Panthera tigris altaica*), for example, get along quite nicely in the deep snow and frigid temperatures of the Siberian region of northeast Russia (another common name for these cats is Siberian tiger) and China. At the other climate extreme are Bengal tigers (*Panthera tigris tigris*). They are very much at home in the sweltering heat of India and neighboring areas of south-central Asia.

You might think different environments affect the physical appearance of different types of tigers; however, tigers that live in

All tigers, including the Bengal tiger (*shown above*), are in danger of becoming extinct.

different places look fairly similar. Although Amur tigers are considered the biggest of the tiger clan, Bengal tigers can be almost as long as their cousins—more than nine feet from the nose to the tip of the tail—and just about as heavy, weighing more than four hundred pounds. One difference between the two is in their coats. Amur tigers have pale coats with brown stripes, and they grow long, shaggy fur in the winter; Bengal tigers have black stripes against light- to reddish-yellow coats.

Despite their great size and strength, all tiger species are in danger of becoming extinct within your lifetime. Unfortunately, three tiger subspecies have already gone the way of the saber-toothed cats. Caspian tigers (*Panthera tigris virgata*), Javan tigers (*Panthera tigris sondaica*), and Bali tigers (*Panthera tigris balica*) went extinct during the twentieth century. Scientists are trying to figure out how to save four of the remaining five subspecies of tigers that are clinging to survival by a claw.

Sadly, it may already be too late for at least one of those subspecies. Most experts are convinced that South China tigers (*Panthera tigris amoyensis*) are already extinct in the wild. To make matters worse, only a handful of them are living in zoos. Amur and Sumatran tigers (*Panthera tigris sumatrae*) probably number no more than four hundred each, and about one thousand Indo-Chinese tigers (*Panthera tigris corbetti*)

Surprisingly, white tigers are a color variation of the Bengal tiger, not the Amur tiger. As you might expect, white tigers (which have gorgeous blue eyes) make an easy target for hunters, so none have been seen in the wild since the 1950s.

may still be roaming freely over their huge geographic range.

It's hard to believe that all tiger subspecies are in deep trouble, even Bengal tigers, which may number several thousand. Tigers are endangered for three main reasons. First, their habitat is rapidly disappearing, making their survival more difficult. As a result, many are killed because they eat livestock when their natural prey becomes scarce. Finally, they're killed because their fur, teeth, claws, and other parts are in demand in a booming illegal trade business, known as a black market.

STEALTHY HUNTER: THE LEOPARD

Wild cats can be some of the most ferocious predators on Earth, and one of the most frightening night stalkers is found in Asia and Africa: the leopard (*Panthera pardus*). Not much bigger than large dogs, these sly hunters are so strong that they can bring down animals much larger than themselves—such as deer and antelope—and the way they find prey in the dark of night is downright spooky.

Leopards have finely tuned senses that guide them: keen night vision, exceptional hearing, and a terrific sense of smell. And, because wolves and wild dogs are usually lurking nearby and are more than happy to help themselves to the leopard's kill, leopards have developed the ability to carry prey animals, some as large as themselves, up into trees. This mind-boggling combination of strength and agility allows leopards to survive in areas where cats their size otherwise might not.

Life is by no means easy for leopards, however. They are in a constant battle with other predators for prey animals, but the pressure put on them by people is the greatest threat to leopard survival.

Despite their secretive nature, leopards face the same threats as most other wild cats. With their beautiful coats, leopards are in as much trouble as other spotted wild cats. Experts tell us that leopards are endangered everywhere they live in Asia. Their numbers are falling because they are losing habitat, are being killed for their body parts, are being killed because they kill farm animals, and are disappearing from regions where their favorite prey animals have been overhunted by people.

Awesome Geographic Range

The leopard gets the prize for having the largest geographic range of any wild cat on Earth. At one time, leopards roamed over most of Asia and Africa—that's a gigantic territory! Today leopards can still be found from the extreme southern part of Africa, northward through most of the African continent, east through the Middle East, across Asia Minor, through the Indian subcontinent, across Southeast Asia, up to China, and north to the Siberian region of Russia.

CHEETAHS: FAST AND FURRY-OUS

When someone says "cheetah," do you think "fast African wild cat"? Well, the "fast" part is right. But you might be a little surprised to learn that not all that long ago, cheetahs (*Acinonyx jubatus*) not only lived across Africa, but also roamed the Middle East and parts of Asia, especially India. As a matter of fact, the name "cheetah" isn't an African word at all, but actually comes from the Hindu word *chita*, which means "the spotted one."

For centuries, rulers in Asia and Europe had cheetahs guarding their thrones. Royal cheetahs were also trained to hunt, as dogs are trained by people today to chase down and capture prey. One ancient ruler, the Mogul emperor Akbar the Great, must have really liked cheetahs, because he had nine thousand of them during the years that he was in power. He used the cheetahs to hunt deer and other game animals—and it's probably safe to say that not many of those animals got away!

The story of the cheetah is the same as that of many other wild cats. As the number of people in Asia grew, cheetahs began to disappear from one country after another. By the end of the twentieth century, only about fifty or so cheetahs survived in Iran, the very last Asian cheetahs. In recent years, private conservation groups, including the Cheetah Conservation Fund, have joined the government of Iran to try to keep the cheetahs in that country from disappearing.

The dark fur of newborn cheetahs shows no spots, allowing the cubs to blend into the shadows and providing camouflage. Spots begin to clearly appear at around three months.

Rare Mountain Cats: Beautiful Snow Leopards

If you had to pick one cat for the title of "Most Beautiful Wild Cat," which one would it be? Many would vote for the snow leopard (*Uncia uncia*). Its long, smoky-gray fur is speckled with distinctive black rosettes. Add to that its deep-blue eyes; huge, furry paws; and an extra-long tail that curls around the snow leopard's body like a big old fluffy blanket, and you've got a wild cat that's breathtaking to see.

The snow leopard, also known as "ghost cat of the mountains," is one of nature's rarest and most mysterious wild cats. If you decided to go looking for snow leopards, you'd begin in the rugged mountain regions of Central Asia. You'd be lucky to find one there, though, because so few of them are spread through the world's tallest mountain ranges, such as the Himalayan Mountains. Snow leopards can be found in about twelve countries including India, Russia, China, and Mongolia.

As you might suspect, snow leopards are some of the most agile and surefooted animals found anywhere on Earth. They live in areas filled with rocky cliffs, windswept ridges, and mountain canyons, and they often have to navigate that terrain over snow and ice. These wild cats are extremely hardy predators, capable of climbing some of the world's most difficult terrain while searching for bharal (blue sheep), ibex (wild goats), and other prey animals. Great leaping ability—especially for a stocky cat that may weigh up to one hundred and twenty pounds—also helps snow leopards capture prey and survive in such demanding places.

The cats' coats allow them to blend in

with their rocky, snow-covered surroundings, but snow leopards are hunted and killed for those coats. Scientist Rodney Jackson, Director of the Snow Leopard Conservancy, tells us that there may be as few as 4,500 snow leopards surviving in the wild today. Snow leopards are not only killed for their coats, but their bones are also used in traditional Asian medicines, despite laws that protect the cats in most areas where they're found. Like other wild cats, snow leopards are also disappearing due to people moving into their territory and killing the snow leopards to protect their livestock.

Helping the Snow Leopard

Several organizations are working to keep snow leopards from disappearing. One, The Snow Leopard Trust, started out in 1981 to protect snow leopards and their habitat across Central Asia. The Trust helps solve problems that come up when people and snow leopards get in each other's way. For example, in certain villages in India, a Livestock Insurance Program has been set up to pay families when predators kill their animals. If animal owners are paid money to replace the animals that are killed, they don't have any reason to kill snow leopards. To get into the program, livestock owners must agree not to kill snow leopards or their prey and to set aside land where snow leopards' prey animals can graze.

Another promising program is Snow Leopard Enterprises. The people who live in snow leopard country are usually very poor. To help them make money and at the same time protect these rare cats, Snow Leopard Enterprises provides families with wool-making equipment that allows them to make products from the wool they get from their sheep and camels. The Snow Leopard Trust then sells the wool products in the countries where the people live, in the United States, and around the world through their online Web store. In return, the people who profit from the wool products agree not to kill snow leopards or their prey animals.

Research is another important part of the work of the Snow Leopard Trust. We need to learn a lot more about snow leopards, and the Trust's research projects provide us much information that could help save this species.

FELINE FISHERMEN

Have you ever gone to a stream or a lake, waded into the water, and tried to grab a fish with your bare hands? If you have, you've got a pretty good idea of how hard it can be to catch fish that way. Imagine if you had to do that every time you wanted to eat! Welcome to the world of a small wild cat that is so good at catching fish with its paws that its common name is the fishing cat (*Prionailurus viverrinus*).

It shouldn't come as a surprise that fishing cats are also great swimmers. They are very comfortable diving into a stream or lake and swimming underwater after their prey. These feline anglers can swim fast enough to catch fish because they have webbing between the toes of their front paws, just like otters and beavers!

A fishing cat is a little bigger and stockier than a typical house cat, weighing in at more than twenty-five pounds. It even looks kind of "fishy" with its gray or greenish-brown fur (which isn't particularly soft) covered with black spots that sometimes run in rows along its back and sides.

Fishing cats live in India and Southeast Asia, a part of the world where rice farming is extremely important. These cats lose more and more of their wetlands habitat to rice farming each year. People also hunt them

because they kill chickens and small domestic animals. Even with all that working against them, fishing cats have been able to survive because a large part of their habitat is thick mangrove swamps where people usually don't go.

Pallas' Cats: Nature's Hairy Little Hunters

Picture a small, house-cat-sized wild cat that could be called "a furball with eyes," and you'll have an image of one of the strangest-looking wild cats on Earth—the Pallas' cat (*Otocologus manul*). With long, shaggy, gray or fox-red fur tipped with silver, Pallas' cats are well suited for living in the mountainous regions of Central Asia, where temperatures can drop to sixty degrees below zero.

The Pallas' cat's thick fur coat also makes it look bigger and heavier than its slight five to ten pounds. With flat skulls and eyes placed near the top of their heads, Pallas' cats may look a little weird, but they're perfectly built for peeking over rocks to find small prey animals without being seen. Pallas' cats eat birds, rats and mice, hares, pikas (small mammals related to rabbits), and an assortment of other small mammals.

The bad news is that Pallas' cats are now seldom seen in many places where they used to live. They were hunted for their fur during the twentieth century and still are hunted sometimes, even though they're legally protected over most of their range.

The disappearance of the pikas, which make up a large part of Pallas' cats' diet, is a growing problem, too. Pikas are being destroyed because people think they carry

diseases, and the poison used to kill pikas also kills the Pallas' cats that eat the pikas.

The good news is that Pallas' cats are slowly increasing in numbers in zoos, thanks in part to the work of Dr. Meredith Brown in Mongolia. Dr. Brown has discovered that wild Pallas' cats can't fight off a certain parasite, and the same parasite was attacking newborn Pallas' cats in captivity. Now zoos are protecting the newborns from the parasite, and more of them are surviving.

CATS, CATS, AND MORE EURASIAN CATS

EURASIAN LYNX

Similar to the wolf, the Eurasian lynx lived in great numbers across Europe, but because of hunting and fur trapping, they almost died out in the mid-twentieth century. Lynx have gradually been reintroduced to some areas where they had disappeared, such as Austria, Germany, and Switzerland. They may soon be reintroduced to Italy, France, and Great Britain.

CLOUDED LEOPARD

These secretive medium-sized wild cats are found in the forests of Asia. It gets its name from the cloud-shaped spots on its coat, providing excellent camouflage in a forest environment. Males weigh up to 50 pounds. The clouded leopard spends much of its time in trees. Its very long tail is used for balancing, and specialized ankle joints allow it to climb down trees like squirrels do—head first.

CHINESE MOUNTAIN CAT

Found in the dry, mountainous regions of China, this extremely rare cat hunts at night, feeding on small mammals and reptiles. Its coat is sandy-brown with a very light underbelly. Thick mats of fur cover its feet, protecting them from the hot sand.

IBERIAN LYNX

The Iberian lynx looks like the Eurasian lynx, except that at about 20–28 pounds, it is about half the size of its Eurasian cousin above. As its name suggests, the Iberian lynx is found on the Iberian Peninsula, which includes Portugal and Spain.

MARBLED CAT

This rare, beautiful cat lives in the forests of Malaysia, Sumatra, and Borneo, as well as on some other small islands nearby. Rather than "spots," this cat appears to have dark streaks and blotches, giving its coat a "marble-like" pattern. Weighing about 12 pounds, it is about the size of an average house cat.

BORNEAN BAY CAT

One of the smallest and rarest wild cats, the bay cat weighs about 5 pounds and is about 20 inches long. It is slender and has very small ears and a long tail. The nocturnal hunter subsists on small rodents and birds on the island of Borneo.

RUSTY-SPOTTED CAT

The rusty-spotted cat is one of the smallest of the wild cat species. Weighing about 6–9 pounds and measuring about 17 inches (plus its 7-inch tail), this tiny cat has reddish spots (body)  and stripes (head) over a golden coat. It lives in India and Sri Lanka and hunts birds and small rodents at night.

FLAT-HEADED CAT

This odd-looking fellow is content eating meat or vegetation. The flat-headed cat has small ears and a short tail and legs, but its most unusual feature is its broad, flat head. Its coat is reddish-brown to dark brown, allowing it to blend in well in the forests and scrub of southeastern Asia (often near where humans live), where it feeds on frogs, rodents, sweet potatoes—and the occasional trash-can feast.

LEOPARD CAT

The leopard cat is special because it is the only cat to be used successfully in a hybrid domestic-wild breeding program. The result is a gorgeous and mild-mannered Bengal cat that has its own organi-  zation: The International Bengal Cat Society. The wild leopard cat's exotic appearance and size made it the perfect choice.

ASIAN GOLDEN CAT

Also known as Temminck's golden cat, the Asian golden cat is about twice the size of a domesticated cat, weighing 14–25 pounds. As the name describes, its coat is a deep gold color that fades to white on its belly. This cat hunts during the day in Asian forests and rocky areas from the Himalayas to Malaysia.

JUNGLE CAT

The jungle cat often lives near farms and other places where people live. In  fact, it is possibly one of the ancestors of our house cats. Tabby-like in appearance, the jungle cat hides out in the jungles, woods, scrubs, and marshes of Egypt and southern Asia.

AFRICAN WILD CATS

Wild cats have lived in Africa for millions of years. Today some of the world's largest wild cats—lions (*Panthera leo*), leopards (*Panthera pardus*), and cheetahs (*Acinonyx jubatus*)—call Africa home. But they're definitely not the only wild cats in Africa. Lesser-known, but just as important, medium-sized and small wild cats also prowl African grasslands and forests. They include caracals (*Caracal caracal*), servals (*Leptailurus serval*), African wildcats (*Felis silvestrus*), black-footed cats (*Felis nigripes*), and sand cats (*Felis margarita*).

Each of these cats, large or small, plays its part in helping to keep nature in balance across the African continent.

lion
(*Panthera leo*)

cheetah
(*Acinonyx jubatus*)

caracal
(*Caracal caracal*)

serval
(*Leptailurus serval*)

sand cat
(Felis margarita)

wildcat
(Felis silvestrus)

black-footed cat
(Felis nigripes)

African golden cat
(Profelis aurata)

leopard
(Panthera pardus)

AFRICA'S WILDCAT ROYALTY

The lion (*Panthera leo*) may not be the "king of the jungle" (Remember, that title belongs to the tiger), but it is an awesome beast nonetheless. Standing more than four feet tall at the shoulder, with massive skulls, huge jaws, and thick, muscular bodies, lions are some of nature's most intimidating predators.

Long ago, lions ranged across Africa, Europe, and Asia and into North America, but they have disappeared from most of their former territories. Now, most lions are found only in Africa, while fewer than three hundred Asian lions still survive in the Gir Forest of India. The lions of the Gir Forest have survived because they were given protection in the early part of the twentieth century, and they continue to be protected today.

Because lions are such amazing creatures, they give rise to lots of questions. For example, why are male lions the only cats with manes? Scientists tell us that the mane acts as a signal to other lions. The lion's mane, like the tail of a peacock, helps males get the attention of females and tells them, "Look, I've got the best mane, so I'll make the best mate!" The lion's mane also helps a male lion appear larger and more threatening to scare off other males.

Speaking of warnings and threats, the lion is famous for its roar. This single-most well-known lion sound can reach as far as two miles away! But lions actually make lots of different vocalizations. One is a puffing sound, which is used when lions greet each other. Lions can also hiss and growl—just like your house cat!

You may have heard lions referred to as "man-eaters." There's good reason. Our ancient ancestors probably hid in caves to avoid lions that considered people just another item on their menu. Unfortunately, some lions still attack and kill people today. Healthy lions usually keep their distance from humans, but old, injured, or starving lions will attack people because they can't catch other prey. Those lions are hunted down and destroyed.

It might seem a little rude, but almost all wild cats prefer to live alone—at least most of the time. Male and female wild cats get together for a brief time during the breeding season, but after that the males and females go their separate ways until the next breeding season. When the cubs are born, Dad is usually nowhere to be found, so Mom raises the little ones by herself.

Other than mothers raising their young and the occasional bachelor group of cheetahs (male cheetahs that have left their mothers but haven't found a mate) hunting together, cats are generally loners.

Lions are the exception to this rule. These wild cats live together in a group called a pride. Scientists tell us that lions enjoy many advantages by living in prides. Females can defend a home territory much easier than if they were alone. Within that home territory, lionesses can hunt and raise their young in relative safety. Even more important is the ability of groups of females to protect their cubs from strange males that sometimes wander into the pride's territory. Strangers usually try to kill the lionesses' cubs in order to mate with the females.

A large pride can have as many as forty lions, but an average pride generally has about eight adult females and two or three adult males along with several subadults (kind of like teenagers) and cubs (both males and females). All the females in a pride are related, and they guard the territory. Most males are lucky if they last two years with a pride before being run off, or even killed, by new males.

Females do most of the hunting when prey is small and quick, but males hunt big prey, like Cape buffalo. Either way, the larger males rule over the females at a kill and are able to eat all they want before any females get a chance to eat—even when the kill was made by the females.

CHEETAHS: SPOTTED STREAKS

Most cats are heavily muscled, which allows them to creep up on their prey and leap on the unsuspecting victim from a hiding place. But cheetahs (*Acinonyx jubatus*) are built for speed. With their long legs, a long thin body, an extremely flexible spine, and a small head for little wind resistance, these spotted cats are extremely well suited for hunting on the wide-open African plains. Most other cats are nocturnal creatures, hunting their prey during the dark of the evening, but cheetahs depend on their speed to chase down fast-moving prey during daylight hours.

The odds of a cheetah catching the small to medium-sized antelopes, as well as hares and other prey that it chases, are not as good as you might expect. Since cheetahs can zip along at nearly seventy miles per hour, you'd think that they probably can catch anything that moves. But scientists tell us that cheetahs capture their prey only about half the time. Even when they do make a kill, cheetahs often are so exhausted that they have to rest and catch their breath before they can eat. It's at those times that other animals, especially scavengers like hyenas and jackals, come along and steal the cheetah's hard-won meal.

Losing their kills to other animals is just one problem for cheetahs in their battle for survival. Cheetah cubs are often killed by other animals, especially lions. People also kill cheetahs when they suspect the wild cats have killed their livestock.

CARACALS: AFRICAN JUMPING JACKS

Some of the most fascinating cats in Africa aren't the biggest. The medium-sized caracal (*Caracal caracal*), for example, is the largest of the "small" African wild cats. Male caracals can weigh as much as forty-four pounds (about twice as big as a super-sized house cat), but they're usually closer to thirty-three pounds. They're found throughout much of Africa, in the Middle East (in small numbers), and in parts of western Asia, including India and Russia.

Despite their plain reddish-brown coats, these distinctive-looking wild cats are easily recognized because of their large ears with extremely long ear tufts, similar to the lynx's. For many years, scientists thought caracals were a type of lynx, but recent DNA testing has shown that they aren't closely related to the lynx at all. Caracals have a thin body and extremely long legs. Its back legs are longer than its front legs, so a caracal looks like it's leaning forward even when it's standing still.

Caracals love to hunt in the tall grassy plains and wooded areas of Africa, as well as on rocky hill country. Because of the habitats they hunt in, caracals have developed an amazing jumping ability. These superstar athletes of the cat family have been seen leaping from a grassy hiding place and soaring high into the air to attack a flock of birds taking flight. Slow-motion photography has captured the image of a caracal swatting several birds from the air during a single leap. Few other predators can do that. Caracals usually hunt rodents, hyraxes, and small antelopes, but they have also been known to kill adult impalas, as well as adult female and sub-adult bushbucks.

Like many wild cats in Africa, caracals are often killed by farmers because they eat small farm animals when their natural prey becomes scarce. Despite that fact, caracals are not protected in most countries where they're found.

THE EARS HAVE IT: SERVALS

Caracals aren't the only medium-sized African wild cats with big ears and unbelievable leaping ability. The serval (*Leptailurus serval*) is another athletic African cat with a very distinctive look. The serval has the biggest ears compared to its body size of any cat in the world. Not only are the serval's ears high, like the caracal's, but they're wide and rounded at the top, but without the tall ear tufts.

Why would a medium-sized cat need such gigantic ears? The small prey animals that the serval hunts can easily hide in the tall grass of the African savanna. But the serval's over-sized ears gives it extra-sensitive hearing that allows it to hear the rodents, lizards, frogs, and birds that it usually preys on, even when the cat can't see them. The serval's spotted coat and tawny gold fur, which looks like a cheetah's coat, provides excellent camouflage for stalking prey in yellow grasslands.

Servals have the longest legs of any wild cat anywhere. They have the appearance of walking on stilts. Once a serval finds its prey, it springs into the air and pounces on its victim. Like the caracal, servals can flush birds into the air and grab them in flight.

Like almost all wild cats, the serval's range across Africa is shrinking due to habitat loss and the growth of human populations. While

they may be declining overall, servals are still found in good numbers in many areas. Because they also like to hunt in the reed beds and grasses found near water, preserving wetlands is an important factor in keeping servals around, too.

DESERT DWELLERS: SAND CATS

Sometimes the name people give to an animal really fits. Such is the case with a little desert-dwelling animal known as the sand cat (*Felis margarita*). This tiny predator is found in the hot, dry regions of northern Africa, the Middle East, southwest Asia, and deserts west of the Caspian Sea.

A sand cat looks like a cute little house cat with sandy brown to light gray fur, dark stripes on its legs, and dark spots or striping on the body. Standing only about ten inches tall at the shoulder and weighing a mere four-and-a-half to six-and-a-half pounds, the sand cat looks odd with its flat head, short legs, and long tail.

Sand cats are specially equipped for living in hot places. They have thick fur padding on the bottoms of their feet, and they can survive with little or no water where other animals would perish. Scientists tell us that sand cats get plenty of fluids from the animals they eat. Those animals include small mammals (especially gerbils), birds, scorpions, insects, and reptiles. The sand cat has a special knack for killing deadly snakes.

Because sand cats almost always hunt at night, they have developed ultra-sensitive hearing and terrific night vision that help them find prey scurrying across the sand in the dark. They're also great diggers, which comes in handy when rooting out prey, digging burrows, or enlarging the burrows of other animals.

The sand cat is thought to be one of the least-threatened species of wild cats, although that may change as people study them more. One of the main threats to sand cats is the increase in off-road driving in desert regions.

PINT-SIZED TERRORS: BLACK-FOOTED CATS

When you think of the most dangerous African wild cats, you probably think of lions or leopards. They certainly are two of the most feared predators in Africa. But maybe, just maybe, the most ferocious African wild cat is also the smallest.

Black-footed cats (*Felis nigripes*)—tiny terrors of the Veldt—are dynamite in a small package. A large, male black-footed cat may only reach five pounds (black-footed cats average about three pounds), but don't let that fool you. Local people have developed a healthy respect for black-footed cats. They refer to these pint-sized predators as "ant hill tigers" for their habit of taking over abandoned ant or termite hills and aggressively attacking anything—or anyone—that disturbs them.

Of all the wild cats that live in Africa, black-footed cats have the smallest range. They're found only in the southern part of Africa in South Africa, Botswana, and Namibia. Black-footed cats live in the dry parts of those countries and eat mice, other small mammals, small birds, spiders, and insects, but they can also kill prey larger than themselves, such as the Cape hare.

This cat gets its name from the distinctive black color on the soles of its feet. The rest of the fur of a black-footed cat is tawny-gold in color, with dark brown or black spots that merge to form bands, or rings, on its legs and tail.

We don't know a lot about black-footed cats' status in the wild, but because they're not seen very often, they're listed as endangered. The primary threat to the survival of black-footed cats is loss of habitat due to overgrazing by farm animals. They also die when they eat poisoned bait intended for other animal pests.

AFRICAN WILDCATS: ANCESTOR OF HOUSE CATS

Something is ironic if it's the opposite of what you might expect. One example of this concerns the African wildcat (*Felis silvestrus lybica*). There is a sad irony in the fact that African wildcats may disappear one day soon because of pet cats. Long ago, our domesticated cats (*Felis silvestrus catus*) actually came from African wildcats, and to this day, pet cats—especially tabbies—look a lot like their distant ancestors. In fact, if you were in Africa and saw a pet tabby cat and an African wildcat side by side, you might not be able to tell them apart.

And that's where the trouble begins. So many pet cats live in Africa that they often breed with pure African wildcats. Over time, the domesticated cat genes and wildcat genes will become mixed, meaning there will

no longer be any "true" African wildcats. All that will remain of the African wildcat will be hybrids (cats that are a little of both.)

Another wild cat species found in this part of the world is the African golden cat (*Profelis aurata*). It is a medium-sized wild cat with either reddish-brown or gray fur that can be plain-colored or spotted. African golden cats mainly live in Central and West Africa in rainforests where they prey on duikers (small forest antelope), hyrax, rodents, and other small mammals, as well as birds and fish.

WILD ABOUT CATS: FROM ANCIENT EGYPT TO TODAY

Experts tell us that dogs were domesticated—trained to live with people—at least 15,000 years ago. But it took another 11,000 years to work up the courage to bring cats into people's homes. Today we take for granted that cats make good companions, but when you think about it, it's kind of surprising that people were able to tame them in the first place.

Just like wild cats, our house cats—or domestic cats—have a scientific name, *Felis silvestrus catus*. Look closely at that name, and you'll find a clue about where cats first became domesticated. Around 2000 BC, ancient Egyptians began bringing wild cats into their homes as pets. Those first house cats, African wildcats (*Felis silvestrus lybica*), were slightly larger than our modern house cats. But why did the Egyptians decide to take in these cats?

African wildcats were experts at killing poisonous snakes, and they also gobbled up the rats and mice that were eating the Egyptians' grain supplies. It didn't take long for the Egyptians to figure out that if they started feeding the wildcats, they'd stay around. After a while, the wildcats were invited into people's homes—probably as kittens, because the adults might have been too aggressive—and were fed in return for the cats killing the harmful pests.

By about 1500 BC, cats were found in

This carving shows the reverence Egyptians had toward cats. Worshiped as gods and mummified for the afterlife, cats were much more than pets in this culture. In fact, thousands of cat mummies have been discovered throughout Egypt, including a huge find in the late nineteenth century. More than 180,000 mummified cats were found in one location. (Sadly, the people involved in this discovery did see the value of such a find and shipped the mummies to England, where they were ground up and used as fertilizer.) Other finds were kept safe, though, and today you can see mummified cats on display at many museums around the world.

many Egyptian homes. Egyptian artists even included cats in family pictures that they painted. It wasn't long before cats became important religious symbols. The sun god Ra, for example, took on the form of a male cat in order to battle against the dark serpent, Apep. The goddess Bastet, who protected children, women, and pet cats, became one of the most important Egyptian goddesses. Statues of Bastet show that she had the body of a woman with the head of a cat. The fierce opposite of Bastet was the lion-headed Sekhmet, the goddess of pestilence and war.

As the worship of cats grew, the Egyptians began holding huge festivals in their honor. Cats became so important that when a family's cat died, the cat was mummified and given a ceremony to prepare it for eternity. And you wouldn't have wanted to harm a cat back then. To kill one, even accidentally, was punishable by death.

PURRR-FECT PET: THE HOUSE CAT

In the U.S., dogs have been the most popular family pets from colonial times—until recently. Just a few years ago, cats overtook dogs as the pet most often found in American homes. There are now more than ninety million pet cats across the country, and the number is growing each year.

From tiny hairless cats that look more like cartoon characters than real animals to the large, bushy-tailed Maine coon cats that have the wild look of their ancestors, domestic cats come in just about every shape, color, and personality imaginable.

Over time, cats with similar characteristics were placed into "breeds" of domestic cats. According to *Cat Fancy* magazine, more than fifty breeds of domestic cats currently are recognized in North America. For all the time

and effort that people put into breeding cats, you might be surprised to learn that the mixed breed is still the most popular house cat.

Cats make great pets, but as an owner, you have responsibilities, too. Unless you're planning on breeding a show cat, you should take your new kitty to your vet, have it tested and vaccinated against diseases, and have it spayed or neutered before the pet is of reproductive age (usually about six or seven months). Some owners also have a chip implanted in their pet to help in locating it should the animal become lost or stolen.

WHAT DO YOU CALL A "WILD" CAT THAT'S NOT REALLY A WILD CAT?

A house cat that gets loose and lives in the wild or the offspring of a "wild" house cat that's roaming free is called a feral cat. The Humane Society of the United States wants people to know that many feral cats are former pets that have been abandoned or accidentally became lost after their owners allowed the cats to roam free. And this is not a good thing—for the cat or for society.

Most cats, including those that come from many generations of pampered house cats, seem to know how to keep their claws sharpened for hunting. Still, life isn't easy for feral cats. They can find it hard to survive on their own. Some cats and kittens are hit by cars. Others are killed by wild predators, such as coyotes. Some die of disease, and some even starve to death.

Unfortunately, so many feral cats are running loose today that they sometimes cause big problems for other species. And the problems caused by feral cats aren't just limited to the United States. Feral cats actually can be found in just about every part of the world, and they've adapted to all types of environments: from the frozen Antarctic to blazing hot deserts, and from farms out in the country to huge cities. In the U.S. alone, feral cats are believed to number in the millions.

Every year many birds and other animals are killed by feral cats and by pet cats that are allowed to roam free. In some areas of the world, native birds used to build their nests on the ground—before people and their cats moved in. Since then, feral and pet cats have completely wiped out some species.

To begin to deal with the problem, cat lovers and volunteers have started "trap-neuter-return" programs to help lower the numbers of feral cats without harming the individual cats. Here's how it works. Entire colonies of feral cats are trapped. Then they're spayed or neutered, vaccinated against various diseases, and returned to their outdoor homes under the watchful eye of dedicated caretakers. This way, the cats are allowed to live out their lives without bringing more kittens into the world—and are less likely to be poisoned or killed as nuisances.

Feral Cats Down Under

Feral cats are a big problem in Australia. Before the early 1600s, no cats lived in Australia. Then sailors from Europe began arriving, and domestic cats came along as pets. (Sailors often kept cats as companions for long ocean voyages.) Soon settlers came—and they brought cats, too. Over time, some of those cats got loose and became feral. Many species of native Australian animals in Australia, including small- to medium-sized mammals, reptiles, and amphibians, have been easy pickings for feral cats. Feral cats also contribute to the loss of native wildlife by infecting other animals with diseases. The Australian government believes that feral cats have been responsible for the extinction of some bird species and have also contributed to the disappearance of some small mammal species.

As a result, the Australian government has developed the Threat Abatement Plan for Predation by Feral Cats. It calls for controlling feral cat populations by removing or killing these cats, especially in areas where conservation projects exist to save endangered native species. Because most people don't like the idea of killing cats, another part of the plan encourages other strategies, such as sterilizing the feral cats, so they are unable to produce offspring. As fewer and fewer feral cats are born, damage to wildlife should be reduced.

Exotic and Dangerous

Do you think you'd like to have a pet bobcat or tiger cub? They're really cute when they're little, but when they grow up, they can be downright deadly.

One of the most frightening trends in the American pet industry over the past several years has been the growth of the exotic animal trade. Exotics are wild animals that people try to keep in their homes. Some people do own wild cats, including tigers, lions, pumas, jaguars, and leopards. In fact, the Humane Society of the United States (HSUS) estimates that the number of wild cats currently being held by people in basements, spare rooms, garages, and small outdoor pens is between ten and fifteen thousand!

Very few of the people who own exotic cats have any type of training that would qualify them to properly care for their "pet." To make a bad situation worse, few exotic cat owners have the money it takes to build good facilities to hold the cats—or even to feed the cats a healthy diet. Just to provide good veterinary care for a large cat can cost thousands of dollars each year. There's no doubt that owning a wild cat is an expensive proposition, but more importantly, it can be extremely dangerous.

While some people own bobcats, lynx, ocelots, and other small- to medium-sized cats (which are still dangerous for their size), other people put their lives and others' at risk by raising big cats at home. All too often, stories about people who have been mauled or killed by "pet" wild cats appear in the news. According to HSUS, tigers alone

Don't let these "kittens" fool you. The bobcat (*left*) and ocelot (*right*) are wild cats— even if raised from kittens, they make potentially dangerous pets.

have killed ten people over the past five years, and during that same time period, one hundred people have been injured or killed by large cats.

Sadly, when exotic cat owners realize that their "pet" is more than they can handle or afford, they have very few options for placing the unwanted animal. Most zoos won't take wild cats from private individuals, because they simply don't have the space to keep them. Few good shelters exist for such animals, and most of those are full. Faced with the prospect of being "stuck" with the animal, some owners mistreat their cats or sell them back into the pet market to become someone else's problem.

The situation became so bad that the United States Congress passed the Captive Wildlife Safety Act in 2003. This important act makes it illegal to import dangerous exotic animals from foreign countries or to transport or sell dangerous exotic animals from one state to another for the pet trade. Unfortunately, the act doesn't cover the sale or breeding of exotic animals within state boundaries. The responsibility for doing that rests with each state, and currently only thirteen states completely ban the ownership of large exotic animals, and seven other states have partial bans.

Until laws are passed in all fifty states to ban the ownership of exotic animals, the HSUS and many other organizations strongly recommend that you should never think of a wild cat as a pet. Wild cats should remain in their natural habitat or in zoos that are working for the conservation of the species.

One look at a lion's teeth can remind you that this is a wild cat that has no place as a "pet."

WILD CATS AT RISK

Several species of wild cats are among the most endangered animals on Earth. As more and more people spread out across the earth's surface, fewer and fewer open spaces remain for wildlife. These animals, including wild cats, are simply running out of places to live. As the human population continues to grow, this situation is likely to get much worse.

African cheetahs are among the wild cats that are facing this problem today. Much of the land in Africa where cheetahs have hunted for centuries is now dotted with farms and ranches, and wild animal herds are slowly being replaced by domestic livestock.

When wild prey animals become hard to find, cheetahs kill domestic animals in order to survive. When they do, farmers and ranchers reach for their guns to kill the cheetahs. And that's how the cycle goes, over and over, until cheetahs are eliminated from one area after another. Without the intervention of a conservation plan, it seemed that cheetahs would gradually disappear from every corner of the African continent.

Thankfully, over the past several years, a number of conservation projects have focused on cheetahs and ways to prevent their disappearance.

A mother cheetah and three of her young cubs at the De Wildt Cheetah Center in South Africa.

HELP BRINGS HOPE:
WILD CAT CONSERVATION

Cheetah Conservation Fund

WHAT THEY DO:

Since 1990, Cheetah Conservation Fund (CCF) has been involved in cheetah projects in Namibia and Kenya, and more recently in Botswana, Algeria, Iran, South Africa, and Zimbabwe. The founder and executive director of CCF, Dr. Laurie Marker, explains, "CCF conducts research across the cheetahs' range to help determine the status of cheetahs, to learn how cheetahs reproduce, and to understand how cheetahs interact with their habitat. By learning more about cheetahs, we have been able to design effective conservation programs wherever cheetahs live."

These include the "Livestock Guarding Dog Program." The goal of the project is to eliminate conflicts between livestock owners and cheetahs. CCF places dogs, Anatolian shepherds (known as Kangal dogs in Turkey where they come from) with livestock owners. The dogs, which have been raised for centuries to protect livestock, live with the farmers' herds twenty-four hours a day. The dogs drive off predators, especially cheetahs. When livestock owners use the dogs, they don't lose animals to cheetahs and therefore have no reason to kill the cats. CCF also helps to get laws passed that protect cheetahs and helps raise money for their projects.

HOW TO CONTACT THEM:

www.cheetah.org

Small Cat Conservation Alliance

WHAT THEY DO:

The Small Cat Conservation Alliance (SCCA) was founded in 2002 by Dr. Jim Sanderson, who realized that there was an urgent need for conservation programs to protect the world's small wild cats. As a member of both the Wildlife Conservation Network and the International Union for the Conservation of Nature and Natural Resources (IUCN) Cat Specialist Group, he decided that three important steps would need to be taken if many small wild cats were to be saved. First, scientists need to collect information about exactly where the cats live, how many of them are out there, and what types of habitats they need to survive. Second, conservation organizations need to work closely with local people to be sure that conservation programs will keep on going into the future. And finally, scientists need to make sure that captive breeding of the cats in zoos continues to improve so that there are good, healthy populations of the cats.

Among others, SCCA is trying to help four rare small wild cats of Asia: the Bornean bay cat, the Chinese mountain cat, the flat-headed cat, and the marbled cat.

HOW TO CONTACT THEM:

www.smallcats.org

A rare flat-headed cat peers into a pond.

Andean Cat Alliance

WHAT THEY DO:

High in the Andes Mountains of South America, local people work together to help the Andean mountain cat (Oreailurus jacobita). It may be the most endangered wild-cat species in the Americas, because some people are all too happy to kill this animal for its fur. In addition, these wild cats also suffer when their habitat is destroyed. The Andean Cat Alliance, (AGA—"cat" is gato in Spanish), with money from the Wildlife Conservation Network, an American conservation organization, has been set up to help keep these cats around.

The four countries where Andean mountain cats are found—Argentina, Bolivia, Chile, and Peru—are now working with AGA.

HOW TO CONTACT THEM:

www.gatoandino.org

Siberian (Amur) Tiger Project

WHAT THEY DO:

In 1992, the Wildlife Conservation Society started its Siberian (Amur) Tiger Project in the Sikhote-Alin Nature Reserve in the Russian Far East. By studying thirty-seven radio-collared Amur tigers over the past fourteen years, scientists have gained a better understanding of what these tigers need to survive—and what happens when tigers and people cross paths. Probably fewer than 450 exist in the wild. According to Dr. Dale Miquelle, head of the Siberian Tiger Project, "The ideal strategy for tiger conservation includes working with local people to ensure that their needs are met, while finding ways to save tigers, so that people and tigers can live together peacefully."

Another goal of the project is to increase protected areas for the tigers, because each tiger needs lots and lots of territory to find enough prey animals to survive. Scientists believe that these steps, and a well-trained Tiger Response Team (a group of tiger experts who capture and move problem tigers to areas away from people), will allow Amur tigers to increase in numbers once again.

HOW TO CONTACT THEM:

www.wcs.org/international/Asia/Russia/
siberiantigerproject

Save the Tiger Fund

WHAT THEY DO:

Started in 1995 by the National Fish and Wildlife Foundation and the Exxon Mobile Corporation, the Save the Tiger Fund was set up to make people aware of the scary situation that wild tigers are in and to raise money for projects to help tigers in their fight for survival. Save the Tiger Fund recently began the Campaign Against Tiger Trafficking (CATT). The goal of CATT is to work out a worldwide plan aimed at stopping the poaching and illegal trade that is causing tigers to disappear so quickly.

HOW TO CONTACT THEM:

www.savethetigerfund.org/CATT/

An Amur tiger bursts to freedom after being rescued from a poacher's snare.

AZA's Felid Taxon Advisory Group

WHAT THEY DO:

Zoo workers have a professional organization, the Association of Zoos and Aquariums (AZA), and one of AZA's most important goals is to keep all living things in the world, including wild cats, from disappearing. The part of AZA that's most interested in keeping wild cats around is the "Felid Taxon Advisory Group" (Felid TAG for short). The Felid TAG tries to help wild cats by managing them wisely in zoos, as well as by working on conservation programs for wild cats in their natural habitat.

The Felid TAG is interested in all wild cats, of course, but it has a special interest in working with small wild cats. One strategy they use is called a Species Survival Plan (SSP). An SSP creates a specific plan for managing cats in zoos by figuring out which cats are related to each other, and then by putting unrelated males and females together to have a better chance for healthy kittens when those cats mate. The first small wild cat SSPs were started in 2001. Today five species—the ocelot, fishing cat, Pallas' cat, black-footed cat, and sand cat—are managed by SSPs. Someday SSPs may be in place for all the small wild cats.

HOW TO CONTACT THEM:

www.felidtag.org

The fishing cat is among the cats protected under the Species Survival Plan.

Cincinnati Zoo Crew

WHAT THEY DO:

The Cincinnati Zoo (Ohio) has more wild cat species on display than any zoo in North America. Most zoos have very few small wild cats, but the Cincinnati Zoo has more than ten different species, including the caracal, serval, fishing cat, margay, ocelot, Pallas' cat, pampas cat, sand cat, and Iberian lynx. Besides giving people a chance to see these little-known animals, the zoo also educates the public about the need to keep small wild cats from disappearing. And, most importantly, they've been successful in breeding many of these cats—not a small accomplishment.

Small wild cats don't breed very well in most zoos, so if any of those cats disappear in the wild, there won't be enough of them in zoos to keep them from going extinct. That's why research scientists are working so hard to figure out how science can be used to increase breeding success in these species. Tucked away in a little corner of the Cincinnati Zoo is an extremely up-to-date research facility that may hold the key. The Lindner Center for Conservation and Research of Endangered Wildlife (CREW) is a worldwide leader in using science to increase our understanding of how small wild cats reproduce.

Dr. William Swanson, director of animal research at CREW, and one of the chairmen of the AZA's Felid TAG, is deeply involved in the study of small wildcat reproduction. He explains, "By using techniques such as artificial insemination, we have been successful in producing offspring from small wild cats."

It works like this: Genetic material (sperm) is collected from a male ocelot in South America. It's frozen and then flown to CREW in Cincinnati. There the sperm is thawed and placed in a female ocelot from the zoo's collection. When the female ocelot has kittens, a remarkable twenty-first-century reproductive technique has been successfully used to help increase the number of ocelots in the world.

One of CREW's most important goals is to increase breeding success in the five small cat SSP species—the ocelot, fishing cat, Pallas' cat, black-footed cat, and sand cat. And they're making progress. Hopefully, within the next few years, all five SSP small cat species will have good, healthy populations in zoos, and, if needed, some of those cats can be put back into the wild to build up the wild populations once again.

MORE OF WHAT THEY DO:

The Cincinnati Zoo/CREW is also involved in several small wildcat conservation projects. One of the most successful is the project to keep ocelots from disappearing in Brazil. The southern Brazilian subspecies of the ocelot (Leopardus pardalis mitis) is only found in the rainforests of southern Brazil, northern Argentina, and Paraguay. To make sure that these cats survive, the Ocelot SSP, ten U.S. zoos (including the Cincinnati Zoo), and a Brazilian conservation organization, the Associação Mata Ciliar, have joined together to form the Brazilian Ocelot Consortium (BOC). BOC provides money to train Brazilian people to work on the project, increase captive breeding success of Brazilian ocelots in zoos, educate local people about the importance of ocelot conservation, and rebuild lost habitat.

Other important field projects that the Cincinnati Zoo and CREW are involved with include conservation efforts for black-footed cats in South Africa, Pallas' cats in Mongolia, fishing cats in Thailand, and sand cats in Saudi Arabia.

HOW TO CONTACT THEM:

www.cincinnatizoo.org

ACKNOWLEDGMENTS

I would like to extend a very special thank you to the following individuals, without whom this book could not have been written:

Marissa Berryman, Snow Leopard Trust

Laura Lee Bloor, Assistant Editor, CAT FANCY Magazine

Christine Breitenmoser, Eurasian Lynx Group

Meredith Brown, DVM, Department of Fisheries and Wildlife, Michigan State University

Richard H. Farinato, Director, Cleveland Amory Black Beauty Ranch

Andy Fisher, head of Wildlife Crime Unit, Metropolitan Police Service, London, UK

Robert M. Hunt, Jr., Curator, University of Nebraska State Museum

Luke Hunter, Ph.D., Wildlife Conservation Society–International, Great Cats Program

Rodney Jackson, Ph.D., Director, Snow Leopard Conservancy

Julie Levy, DVM, Ph.D., ACVIM, College of Veterinary Medicine, University of Florida

Mark Lotz, panther biologist, Florida Fish & Wildlife Conservation Commission, Naples Field Office

Matthew Lovallo, Ph.D., Pennsylvania Game Commission

Jaromir Malek, The Griffith Institute, The University of Oxford, England

Laurie Marker, Ph.D., Founder/Executive Director, Cheetah Conservation Fund

Thomas M. McCarthy, Ph.D., Science and Conservation Director, Snow Leopard Trust

Dale Miquelle, Program Director, WCS Russia Program, Wildlife Conservation Society, International Conservation

Ron Moen, Center for Water and Environment, Natural Resources Research Institute, University of Minnesota Duluth

Nancy Peterson , Feral Cat Program Manager , The Humane Society of the United States

Alan Rabinowitz, The Wildlife Conservation Society

Tom Rothwell, DVM, Research Associate, American Museum of Natural History

Jim Sanderson, Ph.D., ICUN Cat Specialist Group, Small Cat Conservation Alliance

Christopher A. Shaw, Collection Manager, George C. Page Museum, Los Angeles, CA

Dr. Alexander Sliwa, Curator, Wuppertal Zoo, Germany

Rocky D Spencer, Carnivore Specialist, WDFW

Glenn W. Storrs, Ph.D., Asst. Vice President for Natural History & Science, Withrow Farny Curator of Vertebrate Paleontology, Cincinnati Museum Center

Maartin Strauss, Manager: Field Research and Monitoring, National Wildlife Research Centre, Kingdom of Saudi Arabia

Chris and Mathilde Stuart, African-Arabian Wildlife Research Centre, South Africa

William F. Swanson, DVM, Ph.D., Director of Animal Research, Lindner Center for Conservation and Research of Endangered Wildlife (CREW), Co-Chairman, American Zoo and Aquarium Association Felid Tag Group, Cincinnati Zoo & Botanical Garden

Ronald Tilson, Ph.D., Director of Conservation, Minnesota Zoo

Jay Tischendorf, DVM

David J. Vales, wildlife biologist, Muckleshoot Indian Tribe

Robert J. Warren, Meigs Professor, Wildlife Ecology and Management, Warnell School of Forest Resources, University of Georgia

Peyton M. West, Ph.D., Senior Program Associate, Dialogue on Science, Ethics and Religion, American Association for the Advancement of Science

BIBLIOGRAPHY

INTERVIEWS

August 2005
William Swanson, Ph.D. Director of Animal Research, Lindner Center for Conservation and Research of Endangered Wildlife (CREW), and Co-Chairman, American Zoo and Aquarium Association Felid Tag Group.
Pat Callahan, Head Keeper Cincinnati Zoo and Botanical Garden Cat House.

September 2005
Glenn W. Storrs, Ph.D., Asst. Vice President for Natural History and Science, Withrow Farny Curator of Vertebrate Paleontology, Cincinnati Museum Center.

October 2005
Robert J. Warren, Ph.D., Meigs Professor, Wildlife Ecology and Management, Warnell School of Forest Resources, University of Georgia.
Rachel Benton, Ph.D., Park Paleontologist, National Park Service, Badlands National Park.

April 2006
Dale G. Miquelle, Ph.D., Program Director, Wildlife Conservation Society Russia Program.
Jim Sanderson, Ph.D., Director, Small Cat Conservation Alliance.

ARTICLES

Becker, John. "Cat's Cradle." *ZooLife*. Spring 1992.

_____. "Cats Back on the Island—The Reintroduction of Bobcats to Cumberland Island." Georgia *Wildlife*. Winter 1991.

_____. "Lion Kings." *Wild Outdoor World*. November/December, 2000.

_____. "The Littlest Wild Cat." *Hopscotch for Girls*. Oct/Nov, 2001.

_____. "Spotted Cat Transfer." *Wildlife Conservation*. March/April, 1992.

BBC News staff. "Big cat fur coats found in raid." *BBC News Online*. November 3, 2006.

BBC News staff. "Endangered species items seized." *BBC News Online*. July 7, 2006.

BBC News staff. "Illegal Chinese medicine targeted." *BBC News Online*. November 17, 2006.

BBC News staff. "Snow leopard furs seized in China." *BBC News Online*. August 6, 2007.

Choi, Charles Q. "Dolphin Species Driven to Extinction." *LiveScience*. August 9, 2007.

Marshall, Leon. "Chinese Tigers Learn hunting, Survival Skills in Africa." *National Geographic News*. March 2, 2005.

Mott, Maryann. "U.S. Faces Growing Feral Cat Problem." *National Geographic News*. September 7, 2004.

Netting, Jessa Forte. "Cat Woman's Fast Company." *Discover*. March 2005.

Pacelle, Wayne. "Captive Wildlife Safety Act: A Good Start in Banning Exotics As Pets." *The Humane Society of the United States Web magazine*, 2006.

Rabinowitz, Alan. "Connecting the Dots: Saving the Jaguar throughout Its Range." *Wildlife Conservation Magazine*. Jan/Feb 2006.

Radinsky, Leonard and Sharon Emerson. "The Late, Great Sabertooths." *Natural History*. April 1982.

Springer, Ilene. "The Cat in Ancient Egypt." *Tour Egypt Monthly: An On-line Magazine*. April 1, 2001.

Tidwell, John. "Endangered Cat Is Still on the Prowl." Conservation International. Conservation Frontlines Online.

BOOKS

Alderton, David. *Wildcats of the World*. New York: Facts On File, 1993.

Alvarez, Ken. *Twilight of the Panther*. Sarasota, Florida: Myakka River Publishing, 1993.

Baron, David. *The Beast in the Garden*. New York: W.W. Norton & Company, 2004.

Bauer, Erwin A. *The Last Big Cats*. Stillwater, Minnesota: Voyageur Press, 2003.

_____. *Predators of North America*. New York: Outdoor Life Books, 1988.

Becker, John E. *Returning Wildlife—Florida Panthers*. San Diego, CA: Kid Haven Press, 2003.

Brakefield, Tom. *Big Cats—Kingdom of Might*. Stillwater, Minnesota: Voyageur Press, 1993.

Busch, Robert H. *The Cougar Almanac*. Guilford, Connecticut: The Lyons Press, 2004.

Butz, Bob. *Beast of Never, Cat of God*. Guilford, Connecticut: The Lyons Press, 2005

Caro, T.M. *Cheetahs of the Serengeti Plains*. Chicago: The University Of Chicago Press, 1994.

Danz, Harold P. *Cougar!* Athens, Ohio: Swallow Press/Ohio University Press, 1999.

De La Rosa, Carlos and Claudia C. Nocke. *A Guide to the Carnivores of Central America*. Austin, Texas: University of Texas Press, Austin, 2000.

Dorling Kindersley. *Eyewitness Books: Cats*. New York: DK Publishing, 2004.

Engels, Donald. *Classical Cats: The Rise and Fall of Sacred Cats*. New York: Routledge, 2000.

Etling, Kathy. *Cougar Attacks*. Guilford, Connecticut: The Lyons Press, 2004.

Fergus, Charles. *Swamp Screamer*. New York: North Point Press, 1996.

Hansen, Kevin. *Cougar—The American Lion*. Flagstaff, Arizona: Northland Publishing, 1992.

Hehner, Barbara. *Ice Age Sabertooth*. New York: Crown Publishers, 2002.

Hilker, Cathryn Hosea. *A Cheetah Named Angel*. New York: Franklin Watts, 1992.

Hillard, Darla. *Vanishing Tracks*. New York: Arbor House/William Morrow, 1989.

Hinde, Gerald. *Leopard*. London: HarperCollinsPublishers, 1992.

Horak, Steven, ed. *World Book's Animals of the World Lions and Other Wild Cats*. Chicago: World Book, Inc., 2002.

Jackson, Peter. *Endangered Species: Tigers*. Secaucus, New Jersey: Chartwell Books, Inc. 1990.

Kitchner, Andrew. *The Natural History of Wild Cats*. Ithaca, New York: Comstock Publishing Associates, 1991.

Kobalenko, Jerry. *Forest Cats of North America*. Willowdale, Ontario: Firefly Books, 1997.

Landau, Diana, ed. *Clan of the Wild Cats*. San Francisco: Walking Stick Press, 1996.

Line, Les, ed. *The Audubon Society Book of Wild Cats*. New York: Harry N. Abrams, Inc., 1985.

Logan, Kenneth A. and Linda L. Sweanor. *Desert Puma*. Washington: Island Press, 2001.

Loxton, Howard. *The Noble Cat*. New York: Portland House, 1990.

Maehr, David S. *The Florida Panther*. Washington, D.C: Island Press, 1997.

Malek, Jaromir. *The Cat in Ancient Egypt*. Philadelphia: University of Pennsylvania Press, 1997.

McCall, Karen and Jim Dutcher. *Cougar—Ghost of the Rockies*. San Francisco: Sierra Club Books, 1992.

Montgomery, Sy. *Spell of the Tiger*. Boston: Houghton Mifflin Company, 1995.

Morris, Desmond. *Cat World: A Feline Encyclopedia*. New York: Penguin Reference, 1996.

Natoli, Eugenia. *Cats of the World*. New York: Crescent Books, 1987.

Neff, Nancy A. *The Big Cats*. New York: Abradale Press/Harry N. Abrams, Inc., Publishers, 1982.

Orr, Richard. *Little Cats* (Zoobooks Series), Poway, California: Wildlife Education, Ltd., 1998.

Rabinowitz, Alan. *Chasing the Dragon's Tail*. New York: Doubleday, 1991.

_____. *Jaguar*. New York: Arbor House, 1986.

Robinson, Howard F., ed. *Kingdom of Cats*. Washington, DC: National Wildlife Federation, 1987.

Ryden, Hope. *Bobcat Year*. New York: Lyons & Burford, Publishers, 1981.

Savage, Candace. *Wild Cats: Lynx, Bobcats, Mountain, Lions*. San Francisco: Sierra Club Books 1993.

Seidensticker, Dr. John and Dr. Susan Lumpkin, eds. *Great Cats*. Emmaus, PA: Rodale Press, 1991.

_____. *Smithsonian Answer Book*—Cats. Washington, Smithsonian Books, 2004.

Server, Lee. *Tigers—A Look into the Glittering Eye*. New York: Portland House, 1991.

Simon, Seymour. *Big Cats*. New York: HarperCollins Publishers, 1994.

Sleeper, Barbara. *Wild Cats of the World*. New York: Crown Publishers, Inc., 1995.

Stonehouse, Bernard. *A Visual Introduction to Wild Cats (Animal Watch)*. New York: Checkmark Books, 1999.

Sunduist, Fiona and Mel Sunduist. *Tiger Moon*. Chicago: The University of Chicago Press, 1988.

Sunduist, Mel and Fiona Sunduist. *Wild Cats of the World*. Chicago: The University of Chicago Press, 2002.

Swinburne, Stephen R. *Bobcat: North America's Cat*. Honesdale, PA: Boyds Mill Press, Inc., 200`.

Thapar, Valmik. *Tiger—Portrait of a Predator*. New York: Facts On File Publications, 1986.

Thapar, Valmik. *The Tiger's Destiny*. London: Kyle Cathie Limited, 1992.

Trumble, Kelly. *Cat Mummies*. New York: Clarion Books, 1996.

Turbak, Gary. *America's Great Cats*. Flagstaff, AZ: Northland Press, 1986.

Turner, Alan. *The Big Cats and Their Fossil Relatives*. New York: Columbia University Press, 1997.

Veron, Geraldine. *On the Trail of Big Cats*. Hauppauge, New York: Barron's Nature Travel Guides, 1998.

Ward, Geoffrey C. *Tiger-Wallahs*. New York: HarperCollins Publishers, 1993.

Watt, Melanie. *Jaguar Woman*. Toronto: Key Porter Books, 1989.

Wexo, John Bonnett. *Big Cats* (Zoobooks Series), Poway, California: Wildlife Education, Ltd., 2003.

Wolf, Joseph. *The Natural History Museum Library Big Cats*. USA: Mallard Press 1992.

Wright, Bruce S. *The Eastern Panther*. Toronto: Clarke, Irwin & Company Limited, 1972.

Young, Stanley P. and Edward A. Goldman. *The Puma—Mysterious American Cat*. Washington, D.C.: The American Wildife Institute, 1946.

WEB SOURCES

African Wildlife Foundation
http://www.awf.org/

American Museum of Natural History
http://www.amnh.org/science/divisions/paleo/

American Zoo and Aquarium Association (AZA)
http://www.aza.org

The Arizona Game and Fish Department - Jaguar Conservation Team
http://www.azgfd.gov/w_c/jaguar_management.shtml

Ashfall Fossil Beds State Historical Park
http://ashfall.unl.edu/

Big Cats Links
http://bigcatslinks.ath.cx

Canadian Wildlife Service
http://www.cws-scf.ec.gc.ca/index_e.cfm

Cat Specialist Group/IUCN
http://lynx.uio.no/catfolk/

The Cat Survival Trust
http://members.aol.com/cattrust/index.htm

Cheetah Conservation Fund
http://www.cheetah.org
Cincinnati Zoo and Botanical Gardens
http://www.cincinnatizoo.org/

Conservation International
http://www.conservation.org/

The Cougar Fund
http://www.cougarfund.org/

Dallas Zoo Research Projects
http://www.dallaszoo.com/oth/oth.asp?page=rp#mexico

Defenders of Wildlife - Cheetah
http://www.defenders.org

The DeWildt Cheetah and Wildlife Centre (South Africa)
http://www.dewildt.org.za/

Felid Taxonomic Advisory Group (TAG) of the American Zoo & Aquarium Association(AZA)
http://www.felidtag.org

Florida Panther Net
http://www.panther.state.fl.us/

The Florida Panther Society
http://www.panthersociety.org/

The Hornocker Wildlife Institute
http://hornocker.org

The Iranian Cheetah Society
http://www.iraniancheetah.org
Lion Research Center
http://www.lionresearch.org/who.html

Page Museum at the La Brea Tar Pits
http://www.tarpits.org

Save the Jaguar
http://www.savethejaguar.com/

Save the Tiger Fund
http://www.savethetigerfund.org/CATT/

Saving Wild Places
http://savingwildplaces.com/

Siberian Tiger Project
http://www.wcs.org/international/Asia/russia/siberiantigerproject

Small Cat Conservation Alliance
http://www.smallcats.org

Snow Leopard Trust
http://www.snowleopard.org

Snow Leopard Conservancy
http://www.snowleopardconservancy.org/

Wildlife Conservation Network
http://www.wildnet.org/andean_cat.htm

Yukon Beringia Interpretive Centre
http://www.beringia.com/01/01index.html

INDEX

INDEX